THE

Essen

CAMPERᵥ ᴀɴ

BUYER'S GUIDE

11th EDITION

Daniel Lopez-Ferreiro

*With contributions by
some of our Sussex Campervans family of Owners:*

Ken & Carol	Alan & Sue	Phil & Kim	Reg & Paula
Jenny	Jean	Angela	Suzi
Malcolm	John & Jules	Robin & Alison	Chris
Phil & Jenny	Jeff & Mary	Steve & Birgit	Allan & Mary
Jeremy & Janice	Steph & Chris	Bill & Elsa	Pauline & David
Penny	Nicola	Catherine & Dan	Roy
Mandy & Steve	Geoff & Jane	David & Karen	Bobbie
Sue & Rick	Stewart	Graham	Ian & Liz
Mick	Nikki	Jim & Joy	Alisdair & Natalie
Hugo & Thea	Nick & Georgie	Charlie & Jackie	David
John & Carol	Richard & Hong	Michael	Leanne
Martin & Linda	Heidi	Tina	Sandra

Contents

Lifestyle   9

Will I like it?   9
Active retirement   9
Family fun   11
Family & friends   11
Some 'me' time   12
Get more from a hobby   13
Why buy a campervan?   13

The Vehicle   23

Choosing the right campervan   23
Jargon-buster: coachbuilt, tin-top, hi-top or pop-top?   24
    Coachbuilt motorhome   24
    Panel van conversions   25
    Hi-top campervans   25
    Tin-top campervans   26
    Pop-top campervans   27
Small campers can go anywhere   29
Should I buy a new or preloved campervan?   29
Visit a van converter   30
Peace of mind - security & safety   31
Brand New   32
Preloved   34
    Preloved pitfalls to avoid   34
    Important when buying preloved   35
Automatic or manual gearbox?   39

Photo: Bill & Elsa

Diesel, petrol or electric?   40

Electric campervans   40

Ethical travel - families turn to campervans   42

Campervans' car-like fuel economy   42

Holidaying without flights   43

Owning a Camper   47

Maintenance & safety   47

Campervan seatbelts - requirements   48

Engines, emissions & LEZ   50

Clean air zone   50

Driving & manoeuvring tips   53

Reliability - the mechanical side   53

Servicing & maintenance   54

Campervan insurance   54

Road tax   55

Campervan MOT   55

Protect your camper   55

Aftercare 56

"I bought a campervan for my dog" 56

Keeping dogs safe 57

How to afford a campervan 59

Things I wish I'd known 61

Living 66

Electric - batteries & solar 66

Heating - ways to stay warm 67

Refillable tank or gas bottles? 67

Eco-friendly living 71

Cooking & dining in a campervan 73

Water on tap 75

Large fresh water & waste water tank on board 76

Portable water container 76

The best campervan beds 77

Connectivity & working from your campervan 81

Storage tips 83

Do I need a washroom? 85

No washroom? No problem! 85

Chemical toilets: how to use them 86

The Open Road 90

Epic journeys 90

Heading to Europe? 92

EU rules for travelling by campervan 95

A fine day out 95

Hobbies & interests 96

When will you take the plunge? 101

Dear Friend,

So, you're thinking of getting your very own campervan? I'm excited to know that you're considering joining the growing tribe of people who have made the break with one-size-fits-all package holidays, and instead to invest in a vehicle which can replace a car, and bring relaxation and fun into everyday life.

I'm a campervan expert, having been designing and building campervans for many years. My family and I have been using leisure vehicles for a long time, through the various phases of family life, from when the children were little to the present, now they are grown-up. We wanted to be more free and relaxed, and get away from both the effort and inconvenience of conventional camping, and from the conformity and rigours of 'ordinary' holidays. As our family grew, holidays were becoming more expensive and less enjoyable.

My wife was certain that a campervan was the perfect solution; but I had never been camping as a child. First I agreed to try a trailer tent... breathing in the fresh air, chatting to other campers; this was a good life. We traded up to a caravan, but still watched campervan owners enviously - it looked so easy.

With no hitching up, towing or winding of corner steadies, the smart campervan owners were relaxing with a glass of wine, long before we had finished setting up camp. We finally bought a campervan and travelled all over England, Wales, France and Spain, having so much fun and creating priceless memories.

The children loved the campervan lifestyle, too, and I began to see ways to improve the design of each campervan we bought. Soon, the van conversions turned into more than a side project.

I founded a campervan company, Sussex Campervans, and expansion quickly meant the purchase of our own workshop site. That was more than a decade ago. Now, we specialise in building bespoke campervans to order. We have created hundreds of vehicles for happy customers, who have gone on to enjoy some incredible adventures. I hope that in this guide I can share some of our expertise and experience with you, and perhaps inspire you to join our number as a fellow campervan owner.

All the best,

Daniel

Daniel Lopez-Ferreiro
MD of Sussex Campervans and co-author of Campervan Life

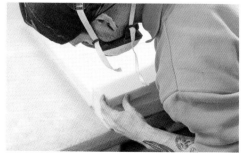

Photo: Phil & Kim

Lifestyle

Will I Like It?

Are you wondering if the campervan lifestyle is right for you? The Pandemic restrictions of 2020 fuelled a boom in camping of all kinds, because people realised it is the safest way to go on holiday, without mixing closely with strangers. In fact, with most flights being cancelled, it seemed like the only holiday option. But if you want to enjoy great outdoors in Britain all year round, a campervan allows you to do it in comfort and style.

Campervan life means you can escape from routine every weekend, even if you work full-time. You can enjoy many outdoor sports and hobbies, knowing that your cosy camper is on hand whenever you start to feel cold, hungry or tired.

With a camper outside your house, you might feel inspired to escape midweek, too. You could just drive to a local hilltop and make a simple supper, or drinks and a snack, watching all of the colours of the setting sun. Or you could park on the seafront and watch the starlings' murmuration aeronautical display, before settling under the pier to roost.

It's an activity that suits all ages and relationships - whether you go with a friend, your spouse, brother or sister, your children or your dog. Many have found that building a campfire, or having a barbecue near the camper is a wonderful way to strengthen their relationships. Best of all, unlike other forms of camping, campervan life can be rather refined and really comfortable - I call it 'camping with standards' - so that it can be suitable for people of all ages and physical abilities.

Above all, what people looking to live the campervan lifestyle tend to have in common is a love of the outdoors and the desire to make the most of their leisure time.

Active Retirement

When you retire, what are your plans? Studies show that some retired people can't decide what to do first, and can spend up to 15 years post-retirement, "reorienting themselves", according to an article on 'How to retire successfully' by The Guardian (2017). One expert, Dr Jonathan Collie,

Early Retirement

Alan and Sue use their campervan for an active retirement with their much-loved Labradoodle, Barney.

Alan says, "I thought about owning a campervan for years before I actually took the plunge. My friend had bought one, and I had decided that I wanted to buy a camper when I retired."

Redundancy suddenly made Alan's plans become possible much earlier than expected, and he says, "I did think about buying a Porsche instead for a while, but I settled on the campervan and it's been the best thing I've ever bought. I love driving it - even if I'm stuck in traffic. The campervan is comfortable and I like being able to see above the cars. Sue loves it too. Our campervan is the best thing I ever bought."

Campervan life can be really sociable, he says. "Our campervan has shaped our lifestyle and encouraged us to get in touch with old friends. We went up to Scotland to see one of my wife's friends who she's not seen for 50 years. It was brilliant seeing them together. Time evaporated, and they are now really good friends again. We would never have done this without the campervan."

Photo: Bill & Elsa

has identified four key elements of a successful retirement, in addition to financial planning:

1. Good social network (beyond family and work).

2. Purpose and mental challenge.

3. Ongoing personal development.

4. Having fun.

Family Fun

When did you fall in love with camping? Many of us enjoyed the outdoor life as children - and now some are passing it on, in style. To a child, heading off on holiday in a home on wheels is magical. Perhaps you have children and wish to introduce them to a healthy outdoor lifestyle - in comfort. Young parents can also enjoy campervan life all year round -using their camper as a cosy place from which to watch their children play football - and then warming them up with a snack afterwards.

Camping, in all its forms, is enjoying a huge boost in popularity both here in the UK and abroad. The number of people saying they camp at least three times a year has increased by 72% since 2014, according to one major international report.

Young people are the biggest group of people going camping and 54% of Millennials are now camping with kids. In fact, camping families with children form the most avid group of campers overall. "Half of all campers say their love of the outdoors is what

Photo: Steph & Chris

sparked their interest in camping. This has remained the leading driver over the last five years. Campers are increasingly seeing camping and other forms of outdoor recreation (hiking, biking fishing, etc.) as one in the same. This trend is being driven primarily by younger campers."

Family & Friends

"The campervan craze is sweeping the globe," according to National Geographic, which offers 13 tips for a perfect campervan camping trip. "Scan through your social media accounts, and you're bound to land on someone's trip through America, New Zealand, or Iceland in one of these converted vehicles. Their popularity makes sense. In these vans, which often feature miniature kitchens, and beds that transform into lounge areas, with folding dinner tables, travellers can enjoy both the comfort of modern luxuries and the freedom of the wild outdoors." Many people travel with friends and family, and the author says, "Bring someone you really like. There's no way around it, you'll be in tight quarters. If you are going on this trip with a partner, family members, or friends, be sure you like them - a lot."

Some "Me" Time

Campervan ownership offers a safe and versatile holiday for single people,

too. Many single people buy a small campervan to use as their only vehicle, thinking they'll mostly use it as a day van, with the odd campsite holiday as a bonus. But such is the freedom of owning a campervan that some seem to spread their wings and head off on very exciting adventures.

Emma Jane Unsworth reveals the joys and perils of solo motorhome travel, in her article for The Guardian (2015): Holidays for one: why I love to hit the road alone. "I've turned down holidays with family and friends to go away alone. Friends have worried that it might mean I was depressed. But depressed is the opposite of how I feel. It's exhilarating feeling self-sufficient, getting somewhere under your own steam."

Get More From A Hobby

Perhaps you have another reason to put a campervan on your wishlist. Once you have a van, it opens up so many great possibilities.

From kayaking, to gardening, to cycling, to mountaineering - a campervan can help you to enjoy your hobbies even more. It's the perfect base to come back to and allow you to spend longer outdoors and travel further.

Why Buy A Campervan?

What's the main reason that all these different types of people buy a campervan? Above all, campervan life makes them happy, as they explain in the article "What's a campervan like to live with day to day?"

Some people buy a camper to recover from illness, divorce, the loss of a friend or parent, or to get their work-life balance back on track. A great many buy a campervan in order to make the most of retirement. Leaving routine behind and heading off in a campervan helps owners to get life in perspective - it's an excellent way to draw a line under the past and move towards a more fulfilling lifestyle.

The flexibility, spontaneity, and range of health benefits that owning a campervan can bring are just a few of the deciding factors that help many people come to the conclusion that campervan life is the next step for them.

Photo: Jenny

Photo: Jean

Photo: Malcolm

Photo: Angela

Going Solo

Some of our friends enjoy travelling solo.

Jenny uses her campervan as a base for archaeological dig weekends, while **Jean** supervises groups of DoE youngsters in the Brecon Beacons.

Angela left her job in hospitality at Gatwick Airport and is now working as a part-time seal warden in East Anglia, staying in her campervan on farms and in wild camping spots at night. She's been a tour guide in the past and loves outdoor life, whatever the weather.

Suzi bought a medium-sized Sussex Campervan and has been recording videos and writing a blog of her wild camping expeditions, visiting a growing list of countries, notably Scotland, Norway, Sweden and Spain. Suzi says, "I've driven 1300 miles in Norway and every one of them has been completely amazing. I am truly living life, in the way I had dreamed. I am facing fears every day, and every day I overcome them."

Malcolm feels that going on holiday with his rescue dog George in the campervan has helped him to cope with the sad loss of his partner of 36 years. He says, "I've never felt lonely. I'm looking forward to being more adventurous this year."

UK Campervan Holidays

John and Jules stayed fairly local for their campervan holidays - and the best thing about it was spending extra time with their grandchildren.

With music festivals cancelled and foreign travel looking risky in 2020, the couple made the most of more local adventures. In August they went camping for a week at Park Farm campsite, near the National Trust's beautiful 14th-century Bodiam Castle in East Sussex. In September, John says, "We took Beano, our lovely little NV200 camper, to Cornwall. We stayed at Trevedra campsite, which I would recommend to others if they are heading down that way. It is a friendly campsite, with very thorough and safely applied Covid restrictions in place. We went in the sea every day and had campfires at night. We also had some lovely walks in the excellent weather along the coastal path around Land's End. Pasties and local cream teas made us feel we were truly on holiday. Despite the current pandemic restrictions. Thanks for building Beano for us. We use it as our second car."

That wasn't the end of the journey for Beano. John and Jules said that since the Cornish trip they have headed northwards. "We stayed in a fabulous Britstop last night - Harefield Hall, North Yorkshire. It is an old monastery, converted to a hotel in the 1980s. We camped for the night in their car park and met their friendly staff when we went in for a great meal and a cosy fire, with a pint and a game of Rummikub! We even went in for breakfast before continuing north to explore the Northumbria coastline. We then went to pick up a narrow boat at Falkirk. Life is good!"

CRAFT BUSINESS ON WHEELS

Alison and Robin sell honey, beeswax candles, bee wraps (to use instead of cling film) and other bee-related products at country fairs around Britain.

Robin says, "I can fit the stand and all the products neatly inside their campervan and once it's all set up at a show we can stay on-site, in the comfort of the campervan. The events are always held in beautiful places, too, so the walk to and from work is a delight!"

When they are not attending craft shows, Alison and Robin use their campervan to drive to Chamonix, in the French Alps, to stay with their son, who is a ski instructor. There's no room for them in their son's flat so they sleep in their Manhattan campervan, just outside the apartment block in Chamonix, at the foot of Mont Blanc.

Alison has a part-time gardening job, and uses the campervan to travel to work. There's plenty of room on board for all her gardening tools, too. And of course it provides a very handy shelter if the weather turns against her during the day's work.

Sea Swimming

Since retiring from the Navy, Chris has been swimming in the English Channel all year round.

He says, "In the winter I fill empty lemonade bottles with hot water from the kettle and spread towels out on the seats and floor of the camper. Then I put the heating on in the campervan before going for a swim with my friends. When I get back I run to the camper, grab the warm water bottles and sluice myself down outside the van. Finally I shut myself inside the warm and toasty 'Beach Hut on Wheels' campervan, wrap myself up in towels and get changed in comfort."

RUBY WEDDING CAMPER

Paula and Reg named their new built-to-order campervan Ruby, to celebrate their Ruby wedding anniversary in 2020.

They had big plans for their special year: music festivals, flower shows and tours of the UK and Brittany. Lockdown postponed some of these plans, so they enjoyed day trips in Ruby the campervan.

"Seaford was a favourite destination, as you can park easily, parallel to the sea front and we had our own loo! There were also great walks along the sea front to Newhaven. We even hung bunting on Ruby to celebrate VE Day," says Paula. "We had a family bubble picnic in Ashdown Forest, too."

As soon as campsites reopened Paula and Reg were off! "At last we could enjoy Ruby the campervan fully.

We ate all meals outdoors, slept well, walked plenty and made the most of the fresh air. This has only whetted our appetite for more trips – next stop Dorset."

Since then, the couple have enjoyed many more trips away including a mid-summer 13 night road trip in celebration of Reg's retirement, across Cornwall and North Devon, stopping en-route in Salisbury to visit the venue where they'd honeymooned 41 years earlier.

Now Reg is retired, the couple have even more time to travel, and are making the most of the flexibility and freedom that Ruby gives them to travel around the country. They embarked on their next trip to Brighton a month later.

Reg and Paula are active members of the Sussex Campervans community and we love that they keep us updated with news of their latest adventures to share in our Campervan Lifestyle magazine.

Our Camper Brings the Circus to Town

It's amazing what you can fit in a Manhattan campervan, and the smooth surface of Ryde Esplanade is a great place for riding a unicycle.

"We belong to a group on the Isle of Wight called Ryde Extreme Performers, which is a circus group," says Jenny. We teach circus skills to people of all ages, at present ranging from eight to over 70! As a group, we also normally take part in many of the carnivals on and around the Island, performing and teaching at a lot of festivals, including the famous Isle of Wight Festival. We have been involved with the group for about fifteen years and we're still learning."

In 2020 the Ryde Carnival and pretty much all events were cancelled due to the Covid-19 restrictions. Jenny says, "We have been practising our circus skills along the sea front with a friend of ours who has the same hobby."

Since retiring from the Fire Service in 2015, Jeff and his friend Ian have become battlefield guides.

"It started as a hobby, then friends from work became interested, and told their friends, and it grew. We don't do it for profit, but our guests do pay our expenses. A lot of people know very little about the two World Wars. I have learned a lot more since I retired.

Before COVID, I spent five years organising trips to Europe for individuals and families. I research their families and regimental history and take them to find their lost relatives' graves, or the battlefields where they fought."

Birgit lives near the North York National Park and loves outdoor activities such as mountaineering, skiing and running - all year round - whenever they get a break.

Her compact Sussex Campervan provides essential shelter, warmth, food and rest to keep her powering up and down the hills. Birgit is an active member of the Mountain Rescue team - so she often takes the camper on call-outs and practice sessions, so that she can take as long as she likes to recover in comfort afterwards.

Birgit also found the CamperCar the perfect place to rest after successfully completing The Great North Run. She has the photo and medal to prove it!

The Vehicle

Choosing The Right Campervan

With so many different options available, it is important to consider how you will be using the campervan, and with how many people. If your requirements should change in future, rather than trading up to a larger vehicle, it would be more economical to simply buy a driveaway awning to increase the living space when you're on a campsite. This could be used as a spare bedroom, with the interconnecting section being an ideal place to use the portable toilet at night.

Before buying your first camper, it is invaluable to visit some quality converters and ask their advice. It may help to draw up a checklist of your main requirements before you go. This might include:

- Number of berths
- Easy-to-convert bed system
- Number of belted travel seats
- Isofix seat belts for small children
- Pop-top roof
- Gas or induction hob
- Sink with running water
- Water container with pump
- Porta-Potti or built-in flushing toilet
- Leisure battery
- LED lighting
- Refillable gas system or electric
- Heating
- Cab air conditioning
- Solar panel to top up leisure battery
- Fridge
- Cab seats that swivel
- A small microwave or grill if there's space
- Easy-to-use control panel
- Good instructions on how to use the camper
- Aftercare

- Conversion warranty
- Vehicle warranty
- Bespoke upholstery and furniture colour schemes
- Personalised exterior decals
- Four-season tyres
- Alloy wheels
- Sat-nav
- DAB radio
- Rear speakers
- Tracker fitting
- Choice of automatic or manual gears
- Choice of petrol or diesel engines
- Choice of engine size
- Barn doors or tailgate
- Accessories (eg bike rack, awnings, fixing points for a dog harness or cage)

Jargon-Buster: Coachbuilt, Tin-Top, Hi-Top Or Pop-Top?

Here's your jargon-busting guide to coachbuilt motorhomes, tin-top campervans, hi-top campervans and pop-top campervans. One size does not fit all - so which will you choose?

Coachbuilt Motorhome

A coachbuilt motorhome is essentially a van chassis, with a big boxy caravan structure built on top. It's usually constructed as a framework made of plywood, with plastic (GRP) panels attached to that, held together with aluminium strips. I call it a 'block of flats on wheels'. You see them driving around, they're very big and angular; they give you lots of accommodation inside, but the down-side is that it's not something you could drive every day. They drink a lot of fuel, too.

We've owned one or two of these large coachbuilt motorhomes and for 49 weeks of the year it is parked up on the drive, gathering moss, while the batteries and tyres go flat. The market for those coachbuilt motorhomes is shrinking rapidly. We soon got rid of ours - and I think a lot of other people have followed suit. Certainly a lot of folk have come to us at Sussex Campervans and said, "We're just not getting the use out of it; it's sitting there burning road tax and depreciating, so we want to swap it for a campervan that we can drive every day."

Some van converters might even take your old car or camper in part-exchange when you buy a new campervan, to help you make the swap.

Panel Van Conversions

Having considered the pros and cons of buying a large 'block of flats on wheels' type of motorhome, how about getting a panel van conversion, instead? What kind of campervan is best for you? There are three main types of campervans for sale - hi-top campers, tin-top campers and pop-top campers. Let's look at each one in turn.

Hi-Top Campervans

If you buy a hi-top campervan, with a high roof that allows you to stand up inside, one of the advantages is that there is no roof to unfasten and put up when you stop somewhere for a picnic or for the night. There's no roof to bring down and fasten securely before you drive away, either. Inside a hi-top campervan, you usually have cupboards all the way up the wall, so you get extra storage compared to a pop-top camper. The whole interior in a hi-top camper feels pretty spacious and airy, offering you plenty of headroom when you stand up.

So what's the downside of a hi-top campervan?

The main disadvantages are that these hi-tops tend to be 2.4 or 2.5 metres high, so they won't fit under the majority of car park barriers with height restrictions. They also have less ventilation than a pop-top camper, which might be a problem for anyone sleeping up in the roof space. Finally, hi-top vans will burn a bit more fuel, because of the wind resistance.

Tin-Top Campervans

You may also find tin-top campervans for sale - but these are essentially panel vans, complete with the original factory-fitted roof.

It hasn't been modified at all, so you can't actually stand up in it. It's a bit like a people carrier with full campervan facilities. So you still have cooking and sleeping facilities, but you just can't stand up inside, whatever you do to it. So that's a cheaper option than a pop-top camper, but it's quite limiting for some people and it might just give you a bad back from stooping. It's probably best used as a day van or a surf van. Quite often people who buy

Allan and Mary bought Janette (the Vanette), a white petrol automatic NV200 CamperCar in September 2018.

EXPLORE MORE WITH A SMALL CAMPER

"We used Janette six or seven times in the first year. During these trips we have learnt how to manage things in a small camper. The NV200 is very easy and economical to drive. It is no wider or longer than a medium-sized car and under 2m high, so we can use it daily. It can get through and into places larger vans can't manage, like the narrow, steep lanes of Cornish fishing villages and places on the Isle of Wight. When we arrived on our Lizard campsite and said we'd followed the satnav through the nearest village, the site owner was amazed; we were the first campervan that had managed the narrow, bendy, very steep hill - we should have used their directions via the top road."

"The NV200 is treated almost universally as car size, which is a great advantage, as the most convenient car parks in the UK and Normandy ban campervans, while those that do allow campers are further out of town - or they exile vans to the far end of the car park. Many ferries also treat Janette as a car and do not put us in with the lorries if there is space on the car deck."

an old panel van and convert it themselves end up with one of these, because they either run out of money or haven't got the skills to remove the original roof and replace it with a strong steel frame and a proper pop-top tent and roof shell that you can clamp firmly shut for safe travel.

Pop-Top Campervans

Pop-top campervans are the most popular type of campervan for sale in Britain today - here's why. A pop-top camper is only a fraction higher than a plain, unconverted panel van, or a tin-top camper when the roof is closed. The fuel economy is pretty much the same, too. Many people choose to use a small campervan with a pop-top roof instead of having a second car - and some use it as their only vehicle.

A pop-top roof lifts up on hinges and has an insulated tent material surround, which usually provides a range of window and ventilation options. The latest Sussex Campervans pop-top roof has a panoramic viewing window to take in the views, ventilation pockets either side, and the option to completely open the tent to give an 'outside-in' feel on those warm, summer days.

WILD CAMPING

Ken and Carol picked up their small campervan in late 2019, and they're still enjoying their many adventures and have now spent hundreds of nights wild camping.

"After a first trial night of wild camping at Firle Beacon in Sussex and a quick stop back home to pick up some things, we headed north. We went to Silverstone to watch the Aston Martin Owners' Club racing and were surprised to find that we could drive up close to the track at Copse Corner for a great view of the racing action."

Photo: Phil & Kim

Small Campers Can Go Anywhere

With a pop-top campervan, you can get under most height barriers at the entrances to car parks. Many pop-top campervans are around 2.04 metres tall, while some small campervans, such as the Nissan NV200 CamperCar, are less than that - at about 1.95 metres tall with the roof closed for travel. This means that with a bit of care you can get under the 2.1 metre (7 foot) height barriers, and into the car park with all the cars. Just make sure the barrier really is at the height it says, in case they have added many layers of resurfacing over the years. Then once you're in the car park you can open up the pop-top roof. It gives you lots of light and air and plenty of headroom when you are standing up to cook, change into beach clothes or move around inside. It is so easy to put the roof up whenever you like - even just for a picnic stop on a day out - or to break up a longer journey into a set of short, relaxed driving stages. When you unfasten the pop-top roof, you can then push it up at the front and the gas struts quickly take over and lift it the rest of the way. Some van conversion companies also offer an electric roof, as a cost option.

With the roof up, now you have plenty of headroom and you can also have an extra double bed in the pop-top roof area at night. This might be a permanently fixed elevating roof bed, or a set of bed boards that you only need to take on trips when you need four berths. The better van converters will make sure that your pop-top roof bed is padded and upholstered for a comfortable night's sleep.

The pop-top tent itself generally will have a mesh or Perspex window to let plenty of light and air into the pop-top roof tent. Some people buy separate pop-top roof blinds to further insulate the pop-top roof tent during winter trips. You can bring the roof down again and secure it in seconds, when you want to drive off again and carry on with your adventure. The other advantage of pop-top campervans is that they have a low profile, making them pretty aerodynamic and fuel-efficient.

Should I Buy A New Or Preloved Campervan?

The age and specification of the base vehicle plays a major role in the price of your campervan - so when you shop around, do make sure you are comparing the vehicles as well as the quality of the conversion work. Some van converters offer a new conversion of an old van, to keep the price down.

Other possible vans for conversion into small campervans might include the old Citroen Berlingo, Ford Partner, Volkswagen Caddy, Fiat Doblo, Renault Kangoo, Toyota Alphard, Toyota Hiace and Citroen Dispatch. Some of these vans are no longer manufactured, in which case you will only find fairly old preloved campervans for sale based on them.

Don't buy a new conversion of a really ancient van, unless you happen to be a good mechanic, or you have deep pockets for repairs. If a retro image is more important to you than a modern driving experience, you might be tempted to look at the very niche Volkswagen T2 Kombi campervans, based on the last vans ever built in Brazil for Volkswagen, in 2013. Volkswagen finally ceased T2 production there, due to new safety regulations that came into force there in 2014. These are more affordable and reliable than the reconditioned classic 1970s Volkswagen campers, which you may see for sale.

Writer Dave Richards owns a classic VW campervan. He says, "No, old VW campervans absolutely don't go on forever - and I can speak from experience. It's much closer to the truth to say that an old VW will keep running for just as long as you are prepared to keep throwing money at it."

He must really love his old VW campervan, since he reveals, "Over the last twenty-odd years, apart from the usual expenditure that goes hand in hand with 130,000 miles of driving, like 3,000-mile interval oil changes, numerous tyres, a couple of clutches and a brake rebuild, I have replaced every single ancillary on the engine. Last year, I replaced the engine itself at 177,000 miles. The curtains and upholstery have been replaced a couple of times, too, as well as the cupboards, the suspension, all of the doors and the bottom nine inches of the bodywork, too. The back bumper is still original, though."

Being such an elderly vehicle, it has unassisted brakes, is noisy and slow on the road, and needs a run-up to climb a hill. He estimates that the fuel economy is 13mpg and its top motorway speed is 55-60mph. Life was slower in 1979, when his VW Dormraker was born.

Modern campervans are light years ahead of those old classic campervans, as he admits. "From the driving seat of a bay, they seem to handle like something from the 1980s science fiction film Tron."

Visit A Van Converter

Often van converters will display examples of their work online for you to see, along with guide prices. There are even campervan video tours of each model on some of the better websites. Campervans sell quickly, so the stock may not be listed in the same way that identical mass-produced cars would be.

When you've had fun exploring online, make an appointment to visit campervan converters. Ask to get inside some of the campervans and try converting the travel seats into a bed for the night. Finally, book a test drive, to help you decide which campervan is the one for you. Remember, you can book a visit and browse the stock several times before making your mind up. Good converters will not just offer stock vans, but will be keen to build you a campervan that really suits you.

Peace Of Mind - Security & Safety

Understanding the importance of keeping yourself and your family and friends safe on holiday is vital when buying a campervan. Consider buying from registered and insured campervan converters. The electrical work should comply with BS7671: 17th Edition wiring regulations and gas installations to Gas Safe regulations. Another safety aspect to check is the roof construction.

You may come across bargain campervans for sale, offered by keen amateur van converters. Some simply use a wooden frame to support the pop-top roof, which would not be safe in the event of a crash. The best campervan builders use a strong metal frame that maintains the van's body integrity to keep you safe. Van converters that build and sell their own campervans directly to the public should provide good after-care and a warranty.

Some companies may even be happy to show you around the workshop during quieter times of the day, and will take pride in building you a bespoke campervan that gives you and your family a luxurious and safe living environment. Comfort is almost as important as safety. Good campervan converters will maintain all functionality, while providing home comforts.

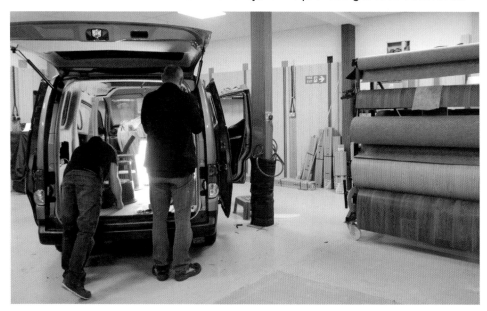

Seats and seatbelts should not only be fitted for safety but also to prevent the aches and pains caused by long journeys. Having comfortable furniture makes rainy day activities inside your camper more of a joy.

Beds and other furniture, such as kitchen cupboards, should be fitted to allow for a spacious living area. This will optimise comfort and allow you to carry out everyday activities such as eating around the dinner table with your family.

Brand New

In 2022 Volkswagen campervans - in fact all new campervans - are safe, reliable, fuel-efficient and low in emissions. They're easy to drive, maintain, and climb hills with ease. Keeping up with the motorway traffic is never a problem, even when fully loaded.

There are some large van conversions based on the Fiat Ducato, Peugeot Boxer or Mercedes Sprinter, or Iveco Daily. These are most commonly used as the base for large coachbuilt motorhomes as well as large van conversions. They use more fuel and take up more width on the road than the smaller Volkswagen T6 campervans, Renault Trafic campers and Ford Transit van conversions.

If you are having a bespoke campervan built to order, it's possible to choose the base vehicle to suit your taste and your budget, subject to availability. For instance, at Sussex Campervans you'll find the Volkswagen T6 panel van converted into the VW Caledonia, the Renault Trafic into the Manhattan or Paradise and the Nissan NV200 into the CamperCar - all available in either auto or manual transmission. The choice is yours.

A brand new campervan is of course the ideal choice if funds are available. Fitted with all mod-cons, beautifully appointed and luxurious, a brand new campervan could cost you anything from £45,000 to £100,000. When you buy a brand new panel van conversion, you can feel safe in the knowledge that the campervan is covered by the manufacturer's vehicle warranty, as well as the converter's warranty. A bespoke converter will buy the vehicle on

Jim & Joy use their campervan to explore the UK, towing their beloved 45-year-old MG Midget behind.

MG RACING

Now retired, Jim and Joy have the freedom to head off on adventures whenever they choose. Jim also owns a beautifully restored 45-year-old MG Midget, which he loves to drive and takes to rallies. The camper's economy is fabulous for towing and provides flexibility while they are away. They can tow the Midget on a trailer, which means Jim and Joy can leave the campervan parked up and explore the local area in the Midget. On MG race days, Jim arrives early and spends the night in his campervan, so he's properly refreshed before hitting the tracks.

your behalf and invite you to choose one of their tried and tested layouts, along with the finest upholstery fabric and furniture materials, to deliver something unique that you will feel proud to own.

As with any brand new vehicle, there may be some initial depreciation in value, but this is far less than with a car. If you look after it, your campervan will remain an object of desire - and will be easy to resell when you want to - for years to come.

Preloved

A used campervan is perfect for those on a budget. The lower prices of preloved campervans can be a huge draw for many people, especially first-time campervan buyers. There are lots of used campervan dealers about, selling everything from vehicles with one careful owner, to old vans that have toured the world. Some dealers do offer a warranty, but don't forget that you are buying from a salesman and not a manufacturer. You need to know what to look out for, and avoid buying something that doesn't suit your needs. With a used campervan no extras are available, unless you do it yourself.

Preloved Pitfalls To Avoid

If you decide to start your campervan lifestyle by buying a preloved campervan privately through small classified adverts, you are entering the realm of "Buyer beware" and "Sold as seen" - there will not be a warranty available from a private seller.

Vehicle expert Honest John says, "If the price looks too good to be true, it probably is. Some criminals will advertise a camper van that doesn't exist to collect deposits and then disappear. Vans priced below the market value may also be stolen or 'cloned' where they are given the identity of another vehicle that's legitimate."

Before viewing a vehicle it's helpful if you can get the registration number plate and do your own HPI check online to make sure the vehicle is not stolen or written off and has no outstanding finance on it. The AA, RAC and other breakdown services also do these online vehicle history checks for a fee. If you can see a photo of the registration document, this allows you to check that the seller's address matches the one on the document.

Your insurance - or the seller's - may cover you if you do a test drive with the owner's permission. If not, you can arrange a single day's insurance cover.

Important When Buying Preloved

When you go to view a used campervan, Honest John says, "First and foremost, is it used regularly? Campervans are based on commercial vehicles, which are designed to clock up 200,000 miles in a few years, before being sold on or scrapped. They aren't designed to sit unused for eight months of the year. Vehicles that sit around, can be prone to age-related chassis, suspension and mechanical problems."

Low mileage is not always best, he adds. "You should be looking for a vehicle as new as possible for your money regardless of mileage. A four-year-old camper with 100,000 miles is a far better buy than a 10-year-old van with 50,000 miles."

Here are some more things to consider when buying a used campervan privately:

• Ask an expert (a mechanic friend, or the AA or RAC) to do an actual vehicle inspection with you and tell you about any mechanical problems they can identify.

- Honest John says, "Visit in daylight, rather than at night when you might miss damage. If it's raining, ask to drive the van to a filling station forecourt where you can inspect it in the dry, as water can hide bodywork faults.

- "Open the bonnet and check all the fluids. You want to look at the oil on the end of the dipstick. Is it up to the mark? What colour is it? Castor-oil yellow is excellent, light brown is good, dark brown is okay but a tar-like black in a petrol engine spells disaster." He has more advice on spotting potential engine problems, too - from "mayonnaise" in the oil cap to oil on the drive and a leak from the timing belt cover.

- Check the paperwork carefully for MOT advisories and any service history. Honest John says you should look at the actual bills for all the work that has been done on the van in the past. He points out that if the van has a timing belt, rather than a chain, this should be replaced every 60,000 miles or four years, whichever comes first. Some vans will go to 80,000 miles, so check the service schedule for that van.

- Walk inside the vehicle, checking for any signs of water ingress - this is crucial. If the floor feels bouncy in one spot, it might mean there has been water damage –

walk away.

- Walk all round the outside checking for any accidental damage to the bodywork, wheels, wheel-arches, door closing operation - and ask how any damage occurred.

- Check the tyre tread. Honest John says, "Uneven wear may be due to incorrect alignment, or it may be due to bent suspension components from kerbs, potholes or road humps. Be particularly wary of uneven front tyre wear."

- Check the back door area for water leaks, which may show up as stains. Honest John says, "Peel back bits of rubber trim and look for 'tide marks' underneath, open and close all the doors and check for even shut lines."

- If there's a pop-top roof tent, put it up and check for mould and any holes in the fabric. Operate the zips to make sure they still work.

- Convert the seats to beds and back again, to make sure you can do it.

- Try out any swivel seats to make sure you can swing them round and then lock them back into place for travel.

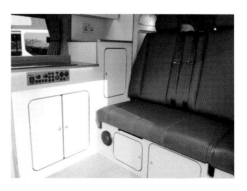

- Check seatbelts for wear or damage.

- Look at the overall quality of the conversion - especially if it was a DIY conversion by an amateur.

Photo: Rick & Sue

- If there is a gas bottle, check that it is in a sealed cupboard and that it can be switched off and secured for travel.

- Try out the hob, heating, water tap, etc to make sure it works.

- Check the electrics work and find the leisure battery to make sure it looks connected up properly, without a jumble of loose wires dangling.

- What type of fridge is there? If it's powered by gas, check that it has a vent to the outside.

If you're happy with the campervan's condition and your research tells you that it's about the right price compared to similar vans for sale, ask for a test drive. Honest John says, "Try every gear, including reverse, the brakes and all of the lights. Also, press every button and switch to make sure they all work and check the air conditioning pumps out cold (and hot) air. Listen out for any unusual noises or clonks."

One lady told us her horror story of buying an old campervan from a small dealer that she didn't know, then finding out that it was unroadworthy, even though it had a new MOT supplied with it. Buying a really old campervan is probably best left to those who can afford to take a risk and who enjoy tinkering with old vehicles.

Most people would rather find a way to afford a brand new campervan, or a preloved camper bought from the original van conversion company, so that they have the peace of mind that comes from a good warranty and aftercare package.

Automatic Or Manual Gearbox?

Most campervans have manual gears, with the gear-stick mounted on the dashboard, which makes for easy gear-changing.

There are also a few campervans with automatic transmission on offer. The Volkswagen T6, The Renault Trafic, the Ford Transit Custom, the Nissan NV300 and the Nissan NV200 all come with a choice of either automatic transmission or manual gearboxes, and with various engine sizes and specifications.

Diesel, Petrol Or Electric?

Traditionally, motorhomes and campervans have been based on panel vans with diesel engines. This is because diesel engines provide the most torque and the best fuel economy when the van is loaded up.

In response to demand, however, there are now petrol and even electric vehicles available for some of the small and medium-sized campervans. For instance, some converters have been able to offer the Nissan NV200 in a choice of a diesel or petrol engine. The diesel NV200 comes with a manual gearbox and a pair of rear doors, while the petrol version has an automatic gearbox and a tailgate.

Renault has launched a version of the Renault Trafic panel van, with an automatic gearbox. This makes it possible to order a brand new automatic campervan from a company that specialises in building Renault Trafic campervans. For instance you could have the classic side-kitchen campervan layout or the contemporary rear-kitchen campervan layout.

A lot will depend on your personal choice, and where you live as ULEZ restrictions are now being introduced in many cities across the country.

Another thing to strongly consider when purchasing a new vehicle is the upcoming ban of petrol and diesel cars and vans from sale in 2030, and hybrid vehicles from 2035 with the aim to be net zero by 2050 (according to Auto Express).

Electric Campervans

Vehicle manufacturers have been working hard to create electric vans that are suitable for more than short inner-city delivery runs, and new models continue to be released. The first to succeed was Nissan, with its little Nissan e-NV200 van. While earlier versions had a limited range, the most recent e-NV200 can cover up to 150 miles before needing to be charged up.

In 2020 Sussex Campervans launched the all-electric e-NV200 CamperCar, which uses no fossil fuels at all, not even for cooking. It's a sophisticated

Photo: John & Carol

state-of-the-art campervan, built to order. The CamperCar has a classic side-kitchen layout and a really easy-to-use 'Rock and Roll' bed. It's wholesome 'green' credentials are second to none. The e-NV200 CamperCar would suit someone who really enjoys life as a journey, exploring each area in a leisurely fashion. As the saying goes: it is better to travel than to arrive.

Over the last couple of years we have seen an increase in electric vans available in the UK. Now, most manufacturers have an electric van on offer and most makers such as VW, Vauxhall, Mercedes, Renault, Nissan and Fiat have taken their existing diesel vans and converted them to electric drive. Maxus has created an electric van from the ground up which isn't related to any other Maxus model. This gives a larger space inside the van making it a great option for a campervan conversion.

Range anxiety is still an issue for most people, but with the introduction of Electric Forecourts across the UK, our clients are enjoying touring in electric campervans and learning to plan their holidays within the battery range.

Campervan life is all about taking the slow and scenic roads, and enjoying the journey, in an easy-to-manoeuvre campervan. But it's also about having a vehicle that you can use as a second car, as a day van, as a base at sports events, and as a spare room when visitors come to stay with you. Whatever you choose must be right for you and your lifestyle.

Ethical Travel - Families Turn To Campervans

As world leaders raise the alarm about climate change, could more families turn to campervans in their search for ethical travel?

A lot of people would love to own a campervan, but worry about the ethics of driving a larger vehicle, amid reports of climate change.

But what are the facts?

Let's compare modes of travel to find out the best ways to go on holiday, as more families turn to campervans. In a recent study, Travel Counsellors of Manchester compared the costs and carbon footprints of various travel modes (see below). Compact campervans would achieve figures close to the 'Car' figures here.

Nice, South of France			
FLIGHT	£854	2 hours	1.3 tonnes CO_2
TRAIN / FERRY	£570	9 hours 40 mins	124kg CO_2
CAR	£576	14 hours	362kg CO_2
Naples, Italy			
FLIGHT	£1142	2 hours 40 mins	2.1 tonnes CO_2
TRAIN / FERRY	£1300	22 hours	198kg CO_2
CAR	£628	20 hours	537kg CO_2
Corfu, Greece			
FLIGHT	£1543	3 hours 10 mins	2.6 tonnes CO_2
TRAIN / FERRY	£1570	36 hours	235kg CO_2
CAR	£1104	30 hours, 30 mins	595kg CO_2

Campervans' Car-Like Fuel Economy

Campervans start life as plain panel vans, designed to carry heavy loads with ease. They nearly all run on diesel, since that gives a van the best fuel economy and torque (pulling power) to go the distance and get up hills.

Quality van converters take the newest and most efficient panel vans and convert them into bespoke campervans. Most of the vans have the latest Euro 6 diesel engines, often with AdBlue to lower the emissions further.

With car-like fuel economy and a comfortable driving experience, our van conversions are more manoeuvrable and cheaper to run than a coachbuilt motorhome - and are far kinder to the environment.

When you look at the fuel economy figures, our campers achieve similar fuel economy to many family cars. We convert the Volkswagen T6 (46.3 combined mpg), the Renault Trafic, Nissan NV300 and Vauxhall Vivaro (all 46.3 combined mpg), as well as the car-sized Nissan NV200 (57.6 mpg for diesel; or 35 mpg for petrol). There are also some electric campervans on the market, offering the greenest holiday yet.

Holidaying Without Flights

As you can see, flying gets you to your destination faster - if you ignore all that waiting around in airports - but dumps an awful lot of CO_2 into the air that we all breathe.

In an article for the Observer newspaper, Muna Suleiman of the Friends of the Earth, suggests that we should all stop flying so much. "Take action to cut pollution by thinking twice before hopping on a plane for your holiday. You might be surprised how many beautiful parts of the world you can reach by train and how relaxing the journey can be – even with children."

Personally, I would not inflict a long flight or a train journey (with several changes) on any family with young children and lots of luggage. I think they'd need another holiday to recover from the experience.

Compare this to campervan holidays, where you just pack all you need in the vehicle, including a few food supplies, and stop frequently to rest, eat and enjoy the scenery.

Most campervan owners have already discovered the stress-free joys of exploring closer to home - meandering through country lanes, rather than blasting down the motorways of Europe.

It's so relaxing that you really don't need to go far to get away from everyday life. And you can turn any spare time into a mini-break, as well as using the van for all your hobbies and activities, all year round.

No wonder more families are turning to campervans in their search for more ethical travel options. Bon voyage!

Photo: Alisdair & Natalie

Photo: Hugo & Thea

If you decide to buy a family campervan, you will be in very good company!

Alasdair and Natalie, ordered their campervan - and then discovered their first baby was on the way. Their daughter Emilia has turned out to be a born campervanner.

"She loves it," says Natalie. "She really enjoys campsites, because she loves seeing all the dogs and smiling at everyone. Lots of people stop and say hello to Emilia and she's not shy. We're still working out the best place for her to sleep as she gets older. She's too small to be in the pop-top roof bed on her own, so she's sleeping with me on the rock and roll bed, mostly."

"Last year we had a three-week holiday in the campervan. We went to the Cotswolds, Lake District, Peak District and Yorkshire. It was fantastic and Emilia was very good. We visited Holmfirth - Last of the Summer Wine country - and Scarborough. Alasdair used the BBQ so we could put Emilia to bed and then cook our evening meal without disturbing her."

Illustrator Hugo and his wife Thea have 2 daughters and a Greyhound, Roller. They use their Manhattan campervan to revisit childhood holiday destinations and make new memories as a family.

When **Nick & Georgie** collected their Manhattan MPV, their first stop was the Isle of Wight. "For our first weekend away in our campervan we took a trip to the Isle of Wight and enjoyed dramatic skies at The Needles. We have learnt that you cannot do without a roll of black bin liners when it's raining for all those muddy and wet items and that there is more than enough cupboard space for a family!"

Photo: Georgie

Photo: Jeremy

Jeremy, Janice and their son Julian use their campervan for outdoor adventures, including windsurfing. Jeremy says, "As a family, we love being outdoors. We always used to go camping, but began getting fed up with being cold and wet in a tent, so we decided to explore several other options. We didn't want a caravan, because I know how long it can take to get a caravan ready to go. That was one of the things that attracted us to a campervan - we knew we could leave it packed, and go when we like. So we decided to swap our car for a campervan. We get away in it just about every weekend. I wouldn't go back to owning just an ordinary car again."

Steph and Chris bought their campervan before starting a family and have explored all around the UK "We first took Maddie away in the camper when she was eight weeks old, and it was so easy. She didn't know any different to being at home, as long as she was warm and fed."

Then along came little Libby. Now Steph says, "We've been in the depths of parenting two very small children and so camping has been way down our list. Today we went 'pretend camping' and it was wonderful. We parked at Box Hill, drank tea, played and cooked dinner."

Photo: Leanne

Owning a Camper

Over the past eight years, sales of new campervans have rocketed, with some estimates suggesting as many as one-in-three new motorised leisure vehicles now being sold are campervans," according to a news story from Out and about Live. They estimate that this is between 4,000 and 6,500 new campervans a year.

"Major survey reveals why campervans are so popular in the UK" proclaims the headline. The survey, carried out by the Caravan and Motorhome Club, with Out and About Live's Campervan magazine, had 1,900 respondents, and provides a valuable snapshot into people's top reasons for enjoying campervan life. The overwhelming reasons people gave were "the passion to escape the everyday drudgery of life and the desire to have the freedom to go where you want, when you want." Almost half of the people surveyed said they do little planning before jumping in their campervan and heading off, preferring instead to "see where the mood takes me".

"Thousands of people have literally turned their dream into a reality with a campervan," said Daniel Attwood, Managing Editor of Campervan magazine. When asked what one piece of advice they would offer to someone thinking of buying a campervan, the most common answer was, "Just do it"!

The Caravan Club changed its name to The Caravan and Motorhome Club a couple of years ago, to reflect the changing membership. Club Marketing Director Harvey Alexander said that the survey results helped them to offer campervan owners "exactly the type of sites and facilities they are looking for." The article estimates that there are more than 225,000 campervans and motorhomes on Britain's roads.

Maintenance & Safety

As with a car, campervans need regular maintenance including MOT's, habitation checks and servicing. You'll also want to make sure that the features installed in your van are safe and legal.

Campervan Seatbelts - Requirements

To keep you and your loved ones safe during the journey, it makes sense for everyone to be wearing seatbelts. It's also a legal requirement, as The Automobile Association explains in its article on Seat belt law and child car seat law:

- Adults: Must wear a seat belt if fitted (cab or rear of campervan).
- Child under 3 years: The correct child seat must be used (cab or rear).
- Child 3 to 11 years and under 135cm: The correct child restraint must be used (front seat) and must be used if seat belts are fitted in the rear.
- A child must use an adult belt in the rear if there is no child restraint and it's a short occasional trip, or if two occupied child restraints prevent use of a third.
- Adults and children aged 12 or more (or over 135cm tall): A seat belt must be worn, if fitted (cab and rear).
- Rear-facing baby seats must not be used in seats with an active front air bag.
- If seat belts are provided, you can't carry more people in the rear than there are seats fitted with belts or restraints.

Good campervan converters will provide proper three-point seatbelts for everyone on board and will have had safety tests carried out on the travel seats by the official VoSA (Vehicle Safety Association) laboratory. If you are comparing campervans solely on price, you may miss the fact that more established van converters have carried out a lot of research and development to keep you and your family safe. Homemade conversions will not have gone through any safety testing.

Parents of small children often ask about Isofix seat belts. A campervan converter will be happy to fit Isofix seat belts where needed. In most campervans there are two or three belted seats for adults in the cab, and two on the rear seat.

For many years some leading manufacturers of large coachbuilt motorhomes provided just two travel seats in some vans. This is something to check if you're looking at preloved campervans and motorhomes, and especially any home-made van conversions.

Engines, Emissions & LEZ

Since April 2019 many cities have sought to improve the air quality for residents and workers. For instance, Central London's LEZ became a new Ultra Low Emission Zone (ULEZ), and this is relevant for motor caravan owners. To drive within Central London's ULEZ, your camper's diesel engine must now be Euro 6 compliant or above (generally, brand new vehicles sold after September 2015).

If your camper is a rare example based on a van with a petrol engine, it must be Euro 4 or above, probably built after 2006. See the Transport for London website to check your vehicle and pay the fees. From 25th October 2021 London's ULEZ area expanded from central London to the boundary of the North and South Circular Roads. This is in addition to the Congestion Charges that apply in the city.

The Euro 6 standard was introduced in September 2015, and all new mass-produced cars and vans made after this date need to meet these emissions requirements. The aim of Euro 6 is to reduce levels of harmful car and van exhaust emissions, both in petrol and diesel. Older diesel vehicles do not comply with this, so if you buy an old campervan you may find you can only enter the zone upon payment of a hefty daily surcharge. This restriction could devalue your investment, so ensure that the vehicle is compliant.

Most dedicated campervan converters will not convert really old vans as they tend to need a lot of work to upkeep, so if you're buying a brand new campervan you should be fine.

Professional converters base their campervans on new, pre-registered (forecourt stock), or nearly new vehicles, mostly with the excellent Euro 6 common rail diesel engines. Today, diesel engines are very refined, and the vans are easy to drive. They are so efficient that it's not uncommon to achieve 35-40 mpg. Vans with petrol engines are much less popular, because diesel engines offer you better fuel economy and more torque, which is what people need from their campervan.

Clean Air Zones

To improve air quality, some local authorities are introducing Clean Air Zones (CAZ), similar to the London ULEZ. Birmingham, Bath and Portsmouth already have the schemes in place and many more cities are rolling them out across the course of the next few years.

The minimum standard for UK clean air zones are as follows:

- Buses, coaches, heavy goods vehicles: Euro 6
- Vans, motorcaravans, minibuses, taxis, private hire vehicles, cars: Euro 6 (diesel) and Euro 4 (petrol)
- Motorcycles: Euro 3

Van Life Matters sums it up as "Generally speaking, if your diesel campervan meets Euro 6 emissions or above (Euro 4 emissions or above for petrol campervans) you will be exempt from charges."

Like many people, Bill & Elsa had only driven cars before...

NEW TO DRIVING A VAN?

"I'd never driven a van before, so I imagined it would be clunky and awkward - even hard to manoeuvre - but I was wrong. Instead, the vehicle we chose was comfortable and I quickly adjusted to the size and placement of the controls. I like having a higher vantage point on the road. I was also surprised that the vehicle wasn't a lot bigger than a large car. My wife Elsa liked it, too.

"We enjoy our campervan enormously and use it a lot to explore the UK. We love all the stretches of Heritage Coast around the country. It's fantastic to park up and take in the spectacular views over a cup of tea. With a campervan it means we're no longer restricted to summer holidays or day trips. Now we can explore further afield, in comfort."

Photos: Steve & Mandy

Driving & Manoeuvring Tips

If you've only driven cars before, you might feel a bit apprehensive about getting behind the wheel of a van. In the past, people used to say you had to be pretty strong to handle a van.

Fast-forward to the present day and the entire picture has changed. Without exception, all panel vans - which form the base for campervans - have power steering. These vehicles boast great visibility - they come with large wing mirrors (some with convex and concave sections that work as blind spot eliminators) and huge windscreens, with a nice high driving position, so you can see the road around you very well. If you are used to driving a car, you'll feel like the king or queen of the road.

Most vans can also be fitted with parking sensors and rear cameras so you really do not have to worry about driving a larger vehicle.

Some people order a campervan with a reversing camera that can be used in place of a rear-view mirror. This is a good idea for families with small children, as well as for solo travellers, who don't have a passenger to help them reverse into a tight space.

It's wise to book a test drive in a campervan - or even just a plain panel van - to boost your driving confidence before ordering a camper.

Reliability - The Mechanical Side

The mechanical aspect of the vehicle is also hugely important. With a brand new vehicle you shouldn't have to worry about breakdowns, MOTs and service history. New vans are covered by the vehicle manufacturer's warranty, typically for the first three years. The best campervan converters also offer a warranty on their conversion work.

With any campervan, to avoid mechanical breakdowns, ensure that you keep the vehicle servicing up to date and check that any previous owner did, too. Check that it has a good mechanical warranty - preferably backed by a third party and applicable nationwide. A van conversion based on a new van will come with the vehicle manufacturer's original warranty. As with any other vehicle, it's a good idea to take out campervan breakdown cover as well, through the AA, RAC, or another provider. If you join through the RAC, it includes membership of the Camping and Caravanning Club for the first year, which gives you access to a huge number of campsites of all sizes, including some attractively peaceful certificated sites, licensed for just five campervans at a time.

Servicing & Maintenance

All campervans should be serviced once a year. Check the manufacturer's specification for your van. The cost depends on your exact vehicle and where you take it; however, you should expect to pay a similar price as for a car. You can get any ordinary garage to carry out the mechanical service work. You also need to check the habitation side, such as the gas, electrics and water storage every 12 months to ensure everything is working safely, with no leaks or damage.

Some converters are able to organise your annual MOT, servicing and habitation check for you, along with any repairs and maintenance, to minimise your time without your campervan.

Campervan Insurance

Instead of car insurance firms, you'll probably find that specialist campervan insurance companies offer the best value – especially if you're not planning to do a really high mileage. Your converter can recommend insurers who realise that campervan owners are a good risk. For instance, you could use Go Compare or another price comparison website to get quotes from motorhome and campervan insurance specialists such as Safeguard, Caravan Guard, Adrian Flux, Comfort Insurance, Saga, and NFU Mutual. It's also worth checking out the campervan insurance provided to members of the Camping & Caravanning Club or The Caravan &

Motorhome Club. Some providers cover you for travel within Europe as well as the UK, and some include roadside assistance - check the small print.

Your quotes may be different from ones given to someone else with an identical campervan, because insurers are also looking at individual factors such as your age, location, expected mileage and how many vehicles you own.

Road Tax

Most van conversions weigh less than 3,500kg and are in the PLG - private light goods - taxation class. Those registered between March 2003 and December 2006, with Euro 4 engines, will be TC36. Vehicles registered between January 2009 and December 2010, with Euro 5 engines, will also be TC36. Older vehicles registered after March 2001 may be TC39. Please see the Gov.uk tax rate guidance for the amount you will need to pay.

Campervan MOT

Panel van conversions under 3500 Kg GVW (gross vehicle weight) all are Class IV, so you can take yours to any garage that does car MOTs (assuming their MOT ramp is of adequate length), and generally it should cost you no extra.

Protect Your Camper

Sadly, luxury vehicles are desirable to thieves. As popularity has soared, so has crime linked to caravans and motorhomes. Scarily, This is Money reported that only 6% of campervans have trackers installed and 45% don't have alarms. When purchasing a campervan, no matter the value, you should think about how best to protect your campervan.

There are many van security devices you can buy to protect your campervan - from cheap visible deterrents, such as a steering lock or a wheel clamp, to a Tracker, supported by an annual subscription. Here is a checklist of security devices you can use to defeat would-be thieves.

- Alarms and immobilisers (factory-fitted as standard)
- Security film for the windows
- Deadlocks
- Steering locks or crook locks

Photo: Nikki

- Wheel clamps
- Gear locks
- Trackers

The best security device of all is a Tracker. Good campervan converters can arrange for a GPS Tracker to be fitted to your vehicle in a hidden place, so that any thieves would find it difficult to disarm it. You then buy a subscription to Tracker, so that in the event of your campervan being stolen you report it to the police along with your Tracker details. This alerts the police to its location very quickly - even if thieves have hidden it inside a shipping container, hoping to sell it on the black market abroad.

Aftercare

Before you buy your campervan, ask if there is any aftercare available from the seller. Good campervan converters will aim to give you a comprehensive after-care service as part of the warranty on their conversion work.

This starts right from the handover, when the converter should spend an hour or so explaining how everything works in your new campervan, encouraging you to convert the bed from a travel seat to a bed and back again, monitoring the leisure battery and vehicle battery charge, using the hook-up lead, and so on. During the handover you should also find out how to secure the pop-top roof, disconnect the electric hook-up cable and turn the gas off before you drive away.

After your session you should be feeling confident enough to get on the road straight away. It will give you peace of mind when you're out and about with the family.

"I Bought A Campervan For My Dog"

We've discovered that people with dogs love campervans - what other vehicle has plenty of room for people, dogs and equipment? And with most campsites welcoming dogs, getting a campervan for comfy camping holidays is the ideal solution.

If your dog is happy travelling in a car, they'll be comfortable in a campervan. In fact, don't be surprised if your dog ends up loving the campervan as much as you do - after all, this is a great opportunity for them to spend more time with their favourite person. You'll tend to be more relaxed on holiday, so your dog will feel more relaxed too.

Keeping Dogs Safe

There are all sorts of ingenious ways to accommodate dogs, large and small, in campervans - because they're part of the family. We've met plenty of dog owners here at Sussex Campervans - and while most are happy to attach leads and dog harnesses to secure fastening points that we can provide in their campervans, others have requested travel crates and cages for dogs in their built-to-order campers.

We've had a few clients ask us to fit strong, lockable dog doors to the back of their campervans. Jenny wanted doors fitted to her NV200 CamperCar Solo so that she could travel more easily with her dogs. She was delighted

LUCIE LOVES THE CAMPERVAN

"We are really enjoying the freedom we get in our NV200."

"We only have to mention the word 'van' and Lucie (our dog) gets super excited and goes and puts herself in her travelling crate. Our first trip after lockdown was to North Cornwall. We couldn't have chosen a better place. We can highly recommend Trewethett Farm CAMC as a base, it has amazing sea views and wonderful sunsets. The coastal path runs through the site, with easy reach to Boscastle and Tintagel."

with the result - and since we were sweltering in record-breaking temperatures on the day she collected her camper, she spotted an immediate bonus. "I can lock the dogs in the camper with the tailgate open, while I dash into the motorway services. They won't get too hot. In fact, we can all sleep securely with the tailgate up at night, to get an extra breeze through the CamperCar."

Another lady, Charlotte, owns Ivy and Wiggie, who compete with the Tails We Win Flyball teams. She takes good care of her dogs and speed champion Wiggie helped the team set a new UK record in 2018. To keep them safe, Charlotte ordered a bespoke Paradise from Sussex Campervans, with large dog cages instead of rear seats. We installed the custom cages, and provided a set of padded roof boards too, so that Charlotte can sleep up in the spacious pop-top roof bed.

How To Afford A Campervan

Phil and Kimberley wanted a campervan, but had no money. Still, they decided to go ahead and look, then find the money, somewhere! They talked about their ideal campervan in great detail, watched lots of YouTube video tours of Sussex Campervans and browsed websites galore. They even made "dream boards" to work out how they would want the interior to look. Then they visualised their ideal lifestyle, with more travel and leisure time.

They were on the brink of ordering a built-to-order campervan, even though they still didn't have the funds, when Phil met a financial advisor. This man looked at Phil's CV and asked if he had any pensions from all the workplaces he'd listed. "Maybe..." said Phil vaguely.

He duly wrote to all his former employers to ask if he had a pension with them - and he discovered that there were no less than seven forgotten pensions! "It was like winning the lottery," said Phil. As soon as he reached 55 he could draw money from one of his pensions - and that was how he paid for their campervan.

There are more ways to fund your campervan lifestyle faster than you might

60

Phil and Kim are "Living, laughing and loving life as we travel full-time in Tut the campervan," and keen to share all the positive things they have learned from divorce in their 40s, finding love second time around, and making a radical lifestyle change in their 50s.

They enjoyed a six-week campervan tour of the Scottish Highlands, before lockdown 2. "What a fantastic experience it has been. Phil found us a beautiful spot in the woods to wildcamp the penultimate night near to The Trossachs National Park. It was frosty so we cosied up in Tut and reminisced about our time here in Scotland," says Kim.

They're now starting their next adventure - moving to Portugal with their campervan and building the next season of their lives together.

think, as we explore in the blog "Still waiting for that lottery win before you buy your campervan?" on our website.

For instance, here are some popular ways to afford van life sooner.

- Part-exchange your car for a preloved campervan - good campervan converters are quite happy to take almost anything with wheels in part-exchange if it helps you to reach your goal.
- Buy the camper on finance. We pay for cars, mobile phones and so many other things using direct debit payments, so why not a campervan? Reputable campervan conversion companies work with independent financial advisors who specialise in finding the best finance deals for individual campervan clients.
- Take out an unsecured personal loan to purchase your campervan.
- Move to a smaller property to free up funds and reduce day-to-day living costs (a popular choice once children have grown and flown).

WE SHARE OUR CAMPER

Our friends Pauline and her brother David bought their blue Paradise Compact camper together in 2016, and named her Joyfree, after their parents Joyce and Godfrey.

Normally they take turns to use the campervan with their spouses. Pauline explains, "We've got a driveaway awning and we have now just bought an inner tent for it to provide more accommodation. My brother and I will cycle the Way of the Roses coast-to-coast cycle route. It's a spectacular 170-mile cycle route, which will take us from Morecambe on the north west coast to Bridlington on the east coast. My husband Jeff and my sister-in-law follow in Joyfree, the campervan."

Things I Wish I'd Known

Many people buy a campervan to aid recovery and make the most of life after difficult illness, or the loss of a loved one. Charlie and Jackie bought their van more than a year ago, to help Jackie recover from a stroke.

Charlie shares his experience of buying the campervan.

"We're very pleased with our Paradise campervan Gloria, as well as the friendly and helpful customer service offered by Sussex Campervans. It's so easy to drive. I enjoy the lovely high driving position, the automatic transmission and 2L engine. The beds are comfy so we slept really well. Best of all we like having mains electricity, so it is home from home. We bought a Nespresso machine, which made breakfast much better."

"We've got Gloria just how we want her. It was hard not to buy too much camping gear too soon. At first we used packing cubes for our clothes in the storage lockers, but they had zips, which Jackie can't open with one hand. So now we have wicker baskets. I bought cheap china mugs to begin with, but now realise Melamine is better for crockery. We are tour-ready at all times."

"Now, 95% of all our trips are in the campervan. Even driving to the park feels like an adventure. Our favourite local place to visit is Seaford. We park

the camper on the sea front and buy fish and chips. The parking is free, and there's no hassle."

"Jackie has lots of physiotherapy and the movement is coming back to her arm and hand. We joined the Caravan and Motorhome Club, because the disabled facilities are excellent. We bought Duvalays for our Paradise beds because they have no zips. Jackie can't do zips with only one good hand, so these are excellent."

"This year our strategy is to go everywhere other people are not going. I have the Caravan and Motorhome Club app so I can book a campsite from my phone. It is free to book and you can cancel up to 24 hours ahead, if necessary."

"Last November I booked all our campsites for Scotland's NC500 route in May. We also want to go abroad when we can, because we have family and friends living in France."

"Our two mottos are: *"Live for the day"*; and *"Don't sweat the small stuff"*."

After they'd been on a few adventures, we asked Charlie how they'd been finding their Paradise Compact Campervan.

"As new campervan owners we really like:

- The super-comfy memory-foam beds (much more comfy than we expected).
- The panoramic roof window (we quickly renamed it 'the bridge'), which was the perfect vantage point in all weathers for watching Cornish surf.
- The longevity of the LPG (we still have all-green lights on our control panel, despite our best attempts to use it up through extensive use of the wonderfully effective heater and hob).
- The really useful storage 'shelf' in the bridge when the roof is up, providing an ideal dumping ground for stuff we couldn't be bothered to put away!
- The quietness and warmth of the van at night, once we'd learnt to close the roof during heavy wind, rain or cold. It was testament to the effectiveness of the wall and roof insulation.
- The under-worktop LED lighting – so funky!
- The 2-litre diesel engine, which goes like the clappers!
- The general quality and craftsmanship of the interior-build and upholstery (several people have remarked on this)."

And was there anything they would change?

- "During the next habitation service we are having extra grab handles fitted to help Jackie climb into the cab.
- Renault's vehicle battery protection timer means that the on-board multimedia stops when you're parked for a while. We'll take a portable Bluetooth speaker with us next time."

Photo: Suzi

Photo: Bill & Elsa

Living

Electrics - Batteries & Solar

Most campervans come with a leisure battery to power the habitation services, such as the lighting, hob ignition and water pump. Motorhome Monthly Magazine, known as "MMM" (2018), explain "The heart of the 12V system, and one of the most important items, is the leisure battery. This is a unit dedicated to powering the living area, not only providing enough energy, but also making sure you do not wake up to a flat vehicle battery and a dead engine." While the system is quite separate from the vehicle battery, the alternator also charges this battery up when you are driving, as it is connected in relay.

The leisure battery is also connected to an electric unit within the outside socket. When you're on a campsite you can use an electric hook-up lead to plug into the hook-up post, just like plugging in an extension lead at home. The power management unit manages that 230V power, keeps you safe, powers all the built-in 12V appliances, LED lights and water pump, while also charging the battery. You can plug items in as well, like phone chargers, travel hairdryers, coffee machines, computers and tablets - though if everything is in use at once, the campsite hook-up point might trip.

A few campervans now offer mains electrical power even when you are off-grid, thanks to the development of exciting new premium Lithium Batteries. It may be worth investing in such a battery (an extra cost option), if you're planning mostly off-grid touring. Having a Lithium battery will enable you to use normal household electrical appliances even when you are not hooked up to mains electricity.

"One relatively recent technical innovation that's been of greatest benefit to motorhoming is LED lamps. These last far longer than ordinary filament bulbs and, importantly, use a fraction of the energy, thus helping to preserve battery power," says MMM. Most campervans come with LED lighting in the habitation area, giving the dual advantage of using very little electricity and also being cool to the touch.

Solar panels get the expert seal of approval in the guide, too, "Another worthwhile upgrade is a solar panel. Fixed to the roof, these help charge batteries by converting sunlight into 12V electricity, controlled by a regulator to prevent overcharging." It is designed to keep your leisure battery topped up when you're camping in the wilds, with no mains electricity. This is an optional extra that owners recommend and can give off-grid power for days at a time before needing to be recharged. As long as there is some daylight, it does keep the fridge, lights and small electrical fittings going for longer.

If you have bought a driveaway awning, you may also wish to consider buying a lantern that will either stand up on a camping table or that you can hang from the ceiling. Some lantern-style lights double up as Bluetooth speakers and chargers for phones and devices, too. Many campervan owners enjoy adding solar-powered fairy lights to their awnings if they are planning to spend a few nights in one spot.

Heating - Ways To Stay Warm

It is worth using the campervan for winter excursions and activities as well as summer escapes. Some owners have even said they find that Winter is the time they use their campervan most It is industry standard for converters to make certain that their campervans are well insulated, both for sound and warmth. Consider also asking them to provide a heater, if this is not a standard feature. There are various types of heaters available for campervans. The most popular is a blown air system, powered by diesel or by LPG. It's quite safe to run the heating at night, thanks to the built-in thermostat. Some converters even mount the heater itself safely below the vehicle, thereby reducing the noise inside the campervan and freeing up some extra cupboard space, too.

When driving, the vehicle's cab heating is useful, because in the UK it is illegal to drive a campervan with the gas heating on in the back. Campervans with an electric hook up or inverter system may benefit from a plug in heater if an inbuilt heater isn't available. These vary in size and can easily be plugged into a 12V or 3-pin mains plug, and provide enough heat to take away the chill.

Refillable Tank Or Gas Bottles

Competent gas engineers must fully check all gas installations to ensure compliance with the appropriate standards, and to safeguard against any leaks. Traditional campervans use a standard gas bottle with a regulator, linked up to the hob and heating. Gas safety regulations state that the gas bottle must be stored in an airtight gas locker, with a compliant vent going straight down through the vehicle's floor. The gas used - LPG (Propane or

Photo: Suzi

Butane) - is heavier than air, so if gas did escape it would drop to the bottom of the locker and out through the vent, away to safety.

The pipework serving the installation should be rigid metal inside the vehicle, where it is then connected to the appliances. Under each appliance there should also be a vent to allow any gas to escape.

In the case of campervans which come with a fixed LPG tank mounted under the floor of the vehicle, this is usually operated via a user-friendly control panel. The advantages of this system are that the gas tank is larger than a traditional Calor gas cylinder, and it can be topped up at any service station offering LPG or Autogas. The appropriate adaptor kit allows for use in the rest of Europe. As a bonus, some campervans with refillable LPG tanks also offer an external barbecue (BBQ) point, so that you can use small portable gas BBQ, which cools down quickly after use, enabling you to pack it away for travel far more swiftly than if you used any kind of charcoal BBQ.

It is a requirement of UK legislation to turn the gas off when driving, for safety reasons. It takes no time at all to switch it back on again next time you want to stop and make a brew. If you are travelling on Eurotunnel - or indeed on a ferry - you must comply with the operator's rules. Contrary to popular belief, there is no issue with either LPG gas bottles, or a fixed LPG gas installation, so long as it is not used for the motive power of the vehicle. Hence, the systems noted above are acceptable, according to current rules in force.

Make sure to check the latest rules on gas prior to travel. At the time of writing, the main points are:

- Gas containers must be switched off whilst travelling and connection systems must be in good condition. Opening the container tap or using domestic services is strictly forbidden until the vehicle has unloaded on the opposite terminal.
- Flammable gas containers may be transported with the following restrictions:
  - Portable containers (cylinders/bottles, etc.): Maximum of 47kg per cylinder and no more than 50kg (99 litres approx.) per vehicle if more than one container;
  - Fixed gas containers (tanks): Maximum of 47kg per container and no more than 50kg per vehicle if more than one container.
  - Fixed containers must be no more than 80% full and will be checked via the gauge or remote indication - if neither are present, the vehicle will be refused.

It's reassuring that ferry and Eurotunnel operators take such care over safety, and provided you buy your campervan from a reputable converter you should find it easy to comply with all these regulations. Some of the best campervan converters have a master switch on the control panel that will turn your refillable LPG gas tank off securely. That is also where you will find the gas gauge, which reveals the quantity of LPG left in the tank. If you have one of the older styles of campervan with a portable gas cylinder, you can usually switch the gas off at the cylinder itself with its built-in regulator, as well as by turning an inline cut-off switch on the gas pipe inside the camper (typically under the sink).

Eco-Friendly Living

Electric campers have become increasingly popular in recent years as we attempt to move towards more sustainable modes of transport. The previously believed myth that buying an electric campervan to help the environment means dramatically sacrificing performance, is finally being debunked. While petrol and diesel van models are still the best option for travelling long distances quickly, buying an electric vehicle is now a viable alternative for those who don't mind making a few pit stops along the way.

In 2020, Sussex Campervans released the first all-electric campervan. This not only has an electric engine, but also has a fully electric leisure system. Gas, petrol and diesel have been entirely eliminated for cooking, lighting, refrigeration and heating, and there's full time mains 230V power whenever you need it. No more filling up heavy gas tanks or hunting around to find an LPG refilling point at service stations - just plug in, charge up and go.

For some, going fully electric just isn't practical yet. There is still a lot of range-anxiety for electric vehicles (with an average of 194 miles on a single charge according to The Energy Saving Trust) and the infrastructure of charging points is still growing. However, there is now a viable option to take a step in the direction of eco-friendly living whilst travelling in a campervan.

Sussex Campervans have taken their well-loved petrol automatic Nissan NV200 with CamperCar conversion and added the same all-electric system, complete with the option of solar panels on the roof. By once again removing the need for flammable gas, this solves multiple concerns about harmful emissions and safety issues while using gas and LPG tanks. With a large Li-Gen battery and inverter, full time mains power can be used off-grid for days at a time without needing to be plugged into an electric hook up. This makes leaving no trace whilst wild camping even easier.

Cooking & Dining In A Campervan

Cooking and dining during a campervan or motorhome holiday can be one of the greatest pleasures – especially when the weather is mild enough for dining al-fresco, pitched up with a beautiful view. Here are the kinds of facilities you will find.

Most campervans and motorhomes come with a twin-burner gas hob and a sink with cold running water, pumped from a simple water container. Some of the larger ones, especially those with a rear-kitchen layout, have enough space for a microwave oven that you can use only when you are hooked up to campsite electrics. And a few have space for a gas oven or grill, or even a full domestic-style gas cooker with hob, grill and oven. Now, the most up-to-date campers may even have an electric induction hob.

In most campervans there will also be a fridge or a coolbox. Some of the older campervan designs have top-loading fridges, which can mean you have quite a bit of rummaging to find the item you need at the bottom of the heap inside. The better campervans have a domestic-style front-opening fridge, so that you can retrieve your food and drink easily. Some campervan fridges also have an ice box (parents will save a fortune if they stock it with supermarket Cornettos instead of queueing for the ice cream van at the beach.)These front-opening fridges often come with a door that you can lock slightly ajar, to keep them well aired if you decide to switch the fridge off between trips.

To make hot drinks you should have the choice of using a kettle on the gas hob, or plugging a normal electric kettle into a socket if you are hooked up

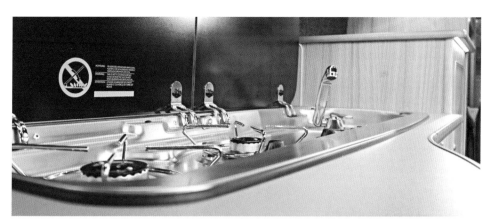

Photo: Charlie & Jackie

to campsite electrics. It's always worth keeping a sealed tin with your favourite hot drinks and instant soups in the campervan, so you can stop on a whim to enjoy a view, brewing a warming drink in minutes. Dining inside the campervan involves putting up a table - usually either a pedestal table with a table top that fits onto one chunky leg that screws into a socket in the floor, or a rail table, which is a table top supported by a rail on the side of the kitchen worktops and a pull-out leg on the other side.

If you have bought a driveaway awning or a canopy/cassette awning to go with your campervan, you may decide to take a camping table and chairs, so that you can set it all up on a campsite pitch and invite friends to join you for a meal in the awning. When you want to go out for the day, you can leave the driveaway awning behind, with your table and chairs set up invitingly for later, also reserving your pitch.

Water On Tap

There are two types of water system; one has a tank fixed in the vehicle, similar to a petrol tank, which you can fill through a cap, using a hose pipe. The other is the lift-out water container system, where you simply take it to any tap, fill it up and put it back in the van. The fixed tank type generally has the water under pressure constantly, whereas with the lift-out canister type you turn the tap, which switches on the pump. Waste water is simply carried through a pipe and let out underneath the vehicle. Sometimes a waste tank is fitted to catch the used ('grey') water; alternatively it discharges underneath. If you don't have a fitted tank, it's a good idea to collect this water in a bucket or similar, so that it can be disposed of at a grey water point.

Which water system is best for you? To help you decide, here are the pros and cons.

Large Fresh Water Tank & Waste Water Tank On Board

- If you have two water tanks, you can have a hot shower in the van.
- It's convenient to have water on tap, wherever you are, for the whole trip.
- You'll need to drive to a motorhome disposal point on a campsite to fill the fresh water tank and empty the waste (grey) water tank properly, due to the quantity.
- Water is heavy, so carrying it in excess can increase your fuel consumption.
- Water from a fixed tank is usually too stale to drink - take bottled water for drinking.

Portable Water Container

- Lightweight and often with wheels, they're easy to fill up with fresh water.
- No real impact on van's fuel consumption.
- It is easy to clean, so the water is fit to drink.
- Waste washing up water from the sink just goes through the waste pipe into a small bucket, which you can tip into the campsite pitch drain, or into the hedge beside the road. Never empty it into a stream or pond.

The Best Campervan Beds

Plenty of campervans are perfect for two, but some sleep four or more. If you choose a campervan with the classic side-kitchen layout, the main bed is generally a double, made from the rear travel seats. There should be room for one or two more adults in the pop-top roof bed. Some parents use the cab seats as a bed for the smallest child, either using a Moses basket or travel cot there, or buying a hammock to suspend across the cab area. If you choose a long wheelbase campervan you may find there is an ottoman bench seat, placed across the full width of the van, behind the cab seats. This makes an ideal bed for a young child, too.

When it comes to making up the main double bed in your campervan, it should be quick and easy. But they're not all the same, so make sure you find out how to do it, and try it for yourself, before buying a camper. Campervans and motorhomes have a variety of different styles of bed. In less fuel-conscious times there was a trend for fixed double beds in large coachbuilt motorhomes. This fashion is passing, since it leaves so little space for a lounge/dining area, unless you're prepared to drive a very large vehicle. Another popular bed layout in the larger motorhomes involves twin bench sofas that face each other. These don't make good travel seats, but when you lift the cushions up you can pull out two spindly legs, reposition all the cushions like a jigsaw, and form a double bed behind the cab. The challenge with this layout is that when the bed is made up, it's a bit tricky to

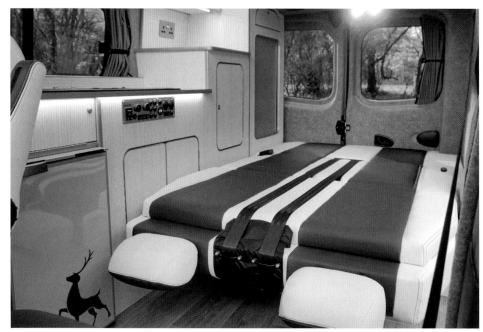

get through the van's sliding side door.

Smaller campervans often have beds that are easier to convert from a travel seat to a double bed or twin beds at night. The smaller the van, the more inventive the designer has to be. Take the classic campervan layout of a side-kitchen and a rear seat that becomes a rock and roll bed, for instance. Many van converters buy in a 'Rib bed' on tramlines and install the kit - job done. This bed looks good and often comes in leatherette, or a dark fabric. Before you buy a campervan with this bed, try converting it from seat to bed and back again. It's more difficult than it looks - and the weight defeats some people.

In a recent Rock 'n' Roll Beds video, Sussex Campervans MD Daniel demonstrates how to convert different campervan beds from daytime to night-time and explains why he designed his own easy-to-use rock and roll bed. He has also designed another type of bed for a more unusual rear-kitchen campervan layout.

The full Paradise Deluxe campervan video tour shows the bed set up at the end. In this layout, the front cab seats swivel to face the rear of the van, while the two rear travel seats slide easily forwards to meet them. These twin beds give you access right through the campervan, from cab to rear kitchen and the back door, at all times. If you'd like a full van-width king size double bed, just use the board-backed infill cushions provided to fill the gap between these twin beds at night.

Plenty of campervans also offer a double bed in the roof. This can be as simple as a set of plain hardboard boards spanning the roof, or can be as comfortable as upholstered bed panels, that you can stack up when you want maximum headroom during the day, then spread out at bedtime or for travel. Another type of roof bed is a built-in elevating roof that goes up with the pop-top roof. You just pull the front edge down to form a sleeping pod at bedtime. Look for a well designed bed, with a flat sleeping surface. Ensure it has the right level of support for your body, especially your back and neck. A good campervan company should encourage you to lie on the bed prior to purchase. Many of our friends say that they sleep better in their campervan than at home.

DOGS NEED BEDS TOO

Penny's living requirements included her dogs, Harry and Jasper, who were competing around the country all year round.

She says, "I used to go to weekend 'Heelwork to music' dog agility and obedience events in a little VW Caddy van with my Westies Jasper and Harry. It was not relaxing setting up camp and packing it all away. Dog events involve long days waiting around and competing, and we all ended up tired. To solve the problem, first I looked at buying a big tent, but then I decided to specify a dog-friendly campervan."

Penny worked with us to design exactly what she needed. Now she has had her Volkswagen Caledonia MPV for two years and it's made events far more comfortable. "The dogs took to the camper immediately. To get them into their crates for safer travelling, I'd encourage them with food treats. They soon jumped in." Penny also uses her camper for holidays and to visit her friends and family.

Connectivity & Working From Your Campervan

Post-pandemic, flexible home working is still an option that many have decided to take hold of. A campervan can be a great location for home working as it enables you to be inspired by your surroundings, find a quiet place to take calls or focus on tasks, or simply allow you to work from wherever you want.

Connectivity is a big factor in a successful home-working (or camper-working) arrangement. Finding a decent wifi connection and phone signal is essential. You can use your mobile phone as a hotspot, however this can eat through your data quite quickly if you are streaming videos or other large amounts of information. A lot of providers now offer cheap 'unlimited data' plans which can allow you to connect devices without a SIM card (like your Kindle or iPad) and use the data from your phone. Make sure you check your plan before using abroad as some networks charge extra for this.

Another option is a WiFi dongle which acts like an internet router you'd have in your home. It looks for 3G, 4G and 5G signals and creates a hotspot for you to connect to. Some dongles will allow you to connect an antenna

WORKING FROM HOME?

Working as a peripatetic NHS clinician means that Nicola spends a lot of time driving to hospitals around Kent and Sussex. On her travels she'd noticed other professionals using campervans as mobile offices and a place to bed down; a home from home. It got her thinking. Could she buy a campervan to use for both work and pleasure?

When she visited Sussex Campervans, Storm Ophelia was about to break. In the half-light a gleaming silver Nissan NV200 CamperCar caught Nicola's eye, and after taking it for a drive, she decided that it was exactly the right size for what she needed.

Like so many campervan owners, she has given her van a name. She says, "Ophelia is really beautifully crafted and lovely to drive. We will be going to work every day round Kent and camping out to cut down my work miles. Then it's back to Sussex at the weekend and up to Scotland for holidays."

which can increase the performance and provide a stronger connection, however this isn't always necessary. You'll need to buy a separate SIM card for this and you can top it up as and when you need it, or treat it like a mobile phone contract.

Of course, some places are so remote, it may be hard to get an internet connection - but that's the beauty of campervan life, escaping the everyday, switching off and being present with your loved ones.

Storage Tips

"How can I pack everything we need for the whole family into a campervan?" One lady who was new to campervans voiced one of the most frequently asked questions when she visited recently. The answer, of course, is not to use holdalls or suitcases, but rather to use the whole vehicle as an enormous packing case. In a side-kitchen layout campervan, you will probably find some cupboards beneath the kitchen sink and hob, plus cubby holes under the rear seats. If you have a long wheelbase campervan there may be a bench seat or ottoman behind the cab seats, and that offers valuable extra storage space.

The 'wardrobe' is usually a small cupboard in the rear of the campervan. There is also more storage space beneath the rock and roll bed, accessed from the rear doors of the campervan. If you have an under-slung refillable gas tank, there will be a cupboard right at the back of the camper, where other campervans would house the gas bottle. There should also be room on the back of the rock and roll bed for bedding or an awning. The rear-kitchen layout campervans generally offer a lot of storage cupboards within the kitchen. They are able to do this because the front cab seats generally swivel round to form the foot of the double bed. This frees up lots more space for storage.

Some small campervans, such as the NV200 CamperCar, naturally have less storage space. The secret of making the most of the storage spaces in your campervan is to buy smaller items and travel light. When it comes to clothes, you need to wash and dry them as you travel, rather than taking separate outfits for each day that you will be on holiday. This way of travelling light works spectacularly well in hot countries.

If you are planning to spend more than a weekend on a campsite, it's well worth putting up a driveaway awning. This will then save your pitch when you go out for the day, and will give you somewhere to store extra camping gear, muddy boots, spare camping chairs, and so on. These items can easily

Catherine and Dan are both teachers, and they enjoy all-weather holidays with their two children.

"With two children, we knew we'd need a fair bit of storage space, so we bought a long-wheel-based Renault Trafic van with a bespoke interior. It's ideal.

Having the freedom to customise the interior to suit our needs was a real bonus. Instead of a cupboard, we ordered a large ottoman. This gives us huge storage capacity and is perfect for storing all the bits and bobs we need when we're away.

We pack a week's worth of clothes and then use the campsite's on-site laundrette when we need clean ones. And everything is kept neat, tidy, and accessible with the help of storage boxes and our fabulous ottoman. "The camper is deceptively spacious. Sometimes it's nice to have some adult-only space, but we've got the awning for that. It makes a nice outside lounge/dining area, and somewhere for the kids to play."

travel in the large foot-well amidships in a side-kitchen camper, or within the kitchen if you have a rear-kitchen camper.

The best type of driveaway awning to buy is an inflatable one - they're so easy to put up compared to awnings with poles. Inflatable awnings are so easy and quick to use that they may even have saved a few marriages...

Other tips our friends have include; packing cubes, investing in the best bedding and learning not to overpack.

Do I Need A Washroom?

Most campervans are converted from panel vans and do not have enough space inside to offer full washrooms. One that does is the new Volkswagen California XXL. The *Telegraph review* begins, "Camper vans are some of the most desirable vehicles we cover on the Telegraph motoring desk. We know this because the web traffic to camper van stories tends to rival that of the supercar reviews, and also because whenever we have a campervan on test, our colleagues badger us to borrow it for a weekend." But it went on to point out that campervan layouts inevitably offer a compromise between home comforts and spaciousness. Based on the Crafter, the VW California XXL is Volkswagen's attempt at bridging the gap between easy-to-drive campervans and huge coachbuilt motorhomes. The Crafter base vehicle is a lot bigger than the VW T6 and similar sized vans used for the majority of campervans. This enables Volkswagen to offer a compact washroom where the whole floor doubles as a shower tray and there is a folding sink in the XXL.

Parkers and Practical Motorhome magazine both reviewed the van favourably, but said that the price might put quite a few people off. Practical Motorhome pointed out that the engine is noisy, and said, "You would really have to be committed to splash out more than £70,000 on a 'van that doesn't include some features you can expect to find in coachbuilt motorhomes at a similar price." At launch, the 600 model with pop-top roof cost from £70,000, rising to £78,145 for the 680 hi-top with 4Motion four-wheel drive. At almost £80,000, VW's largest campervan is competing with coachbuilt motorhomes built on a similarly large chassis, such as the Fiat Ducato or Peugeot Boxer.

These vehicles are too big to drive comfortably through many country lanes in the UK, due to their width: 2.05m (almost 6ft 9ins) - or 2.427m including the wing mirrors. The Grand California XXL 680 is 2.97m (9ft 9in) tall and 6.84m (22ft 5in) long. It's also heavy, at 3880kg MTPLM. Most drivers have just the C1 category on their driving licence, allowing them to drive up to 3500kg vehicles. Smaller campervans are much easier and more economical to drive, which is why they are so popular.

No Washroom? No Problem.

Campervan owners have considered many ways in which they can manage without sacrificing the space needed for a washroom. Of course, the easiest way is to stay on campsites with good hot showers, washing up sinks and laundry facilities. Those who prefer wild camping will typically head to leisure centres or motorway service stations for a shower when needed. Manhattan campervan owner Phil says, "We've joined Pure, a chain of gymnasiums, so we can have a session and end up with a shower there. We haven't needed to stay on any campsites.", while NV200 CamperCar owner Roy says, "The canal marina has excellent washroom facilities, so I use those."

Some campervans do offer the best of both worlds - an easy-to-drive, fuel-efficient campervan with a motorhome-style built-in cassette toilet. Generally these are found in long wheelbase van conversions, such as the Paradise Deluxe by Sussex Campervans.

Chemical Toilets: How To Use Them

Most campervans and motorhomes come with chemical toilets - or with space for one - and it's up to you whether you use them or not. The Camping and Caravanning Club explains the different types of campervan toilets and shows examples of each in its "Getting started" article on toilets.

Popular types of toilets for campervans are the Porta-Potti range by Thetford, and the Portaflush range by Kampa. The advantage of these neat cubes is that they are designed to fit inside a locker when not in use. They consist of two interlocking tanks, with a loo seat and lid on top. Before using the toilet, it's best to prime the base tank with two capfuls of a blue toilet chemical sold widely in camping, boating and hardware stores. Also fill the top tank reservoir with fresh water for flushing, perhaps with some scented pink flush liquid. Eco-friendly versions are available, and are a requirement on some rural sites with septic tanks.

There is a lever at the front of the toilet that opens the trap between the top and bottom sections. It's important to open the trap to let waste flow into the bottom tank when you use the toilet. Push the button on the unit to flush the top section, then close the trap securely. Consider buying quick dissolving toilet paper for use with any portable toilet. It makes the cassette easy to empty, since the paper won't clog the pipes.

The Camping and Caravanning Club article passes on a top tip: "When using your chemical toilet for solid waste disposal, you can help keep the bowl clean by lining it with three pieces of toilet paper, laid out across each other, before use. When the toilet is flushed, the paper disappears into the cassette below with the six leaf-like petals of a flower closing around the deposit." When the lower chamber is full, close the trap, unclip the lower tank and take it to your campsite's designated chemical disposal point (CDP) or Elsan disposal point (EDP) to empty it, or empty it into your toilet at home. Simply unclip the lower tank and carry it to the toilet or chemical waste disposal point, where you can pour out the waste matter in a splash-free manner. Flush and then rinse with the hose provided.

This procedure is the same for both portable and built-in cassette toilets. The latter appear in larger caravans and motorhomes and tend to be made by Thetford or Dometic. Often you can remove the cassette through a hatch while standing outside the van. The larger cassettes usually have wheels and a handle, much like a small suitcase.

The Camping and Caravanning Club advises: "If you can't find an official emptying point, your only option will be to flush the contents of your toilet down a normal WC, which may mean taking it back home. Under no circumstances should you empty black waste (as the contents of a toilet are sometimes called) at a standard grey water ('waste water') disposal point. And always keep it well away from any fresh water point."

Campervan toilets vary slightly, so please read the instructions that come with yours. You may need to empty it every two or three days, if you're not using a campsite. At the end of every trip, empty and clean the cassette, if you've used it.

David & Jennie say their campervan days are simple.

"No need to rush in the morning, a leisurely breakfast, then off for a hike clutching our book of local walks, attempting to decipher the instructions without getting too lost. A picnic on a fallen tree trunk is a highlight. Finally, back to the campsite for tea and Scrabble. Sometimes there is a Zoom call to be joined. It's not a problem with roving internet, and we find the USB charging points in the van useful.

We have fun cooking our evening meal in the Paradise kitchen. The campsite electric hook-up gives peace of mind regarding lights and heat, too. We bought a bijou oil-filled electric radiator and we leave it on all night to take off the chill."

89

Photo: Martin & Linda

The Open Road

There is an element of freedom that comes with having a campervan that is specially designed to your requirements. You know you can do what you want and go where you want, with the added bonus of having all the essential home comforts on board.

If you are new to the campervan lifestyle, it may be worth considering joining The Caravan and Motorhome Club or the Camping and Caravanning Club. They offer you cost-effective access to hundreds of large and small campsites in beauty spots around the British Isles, advice on places to visit, discounts on fuel, activities, campervan insurance, and ferry crossings.

The club campsites are well maintained, with excellent facilities, but can feel slightly regimented. Rules include reversing into your pitch and parking neatly quite close to the electric hook-up point. You're certainly not allowed to hang any washing in the trees on your pitch, either. Consider visiting some club sites to see whether they might suit you before you join. You are permitted to stay on most club sites without joining, but club members do get a discounted rate.

Sussex Campervans keep in touch with people after they've bought their campervans and many owners report that every trip can become a mini-break, whether they are visiting friends, exploring local attractions or even going to summer festivals. Here are a few of the experiences from our owners.

Epic Journeys

Many of our owners mention that they're planning to explore Scotland's scenic NC500 (North Coast 500) route - and quite a few have already done so. Why is it so popular? Many Sussex Campervans have followed the route, which goes from Inverness west to Applecross, then up to Ullapool. It takes in Caithness and John o'Groats, then back to Inverness.

Mandy and Steve, who live in Hampshire, spent three weeks exploring the

NC500 in the campervan we built for them. The camper is based on the Renault Trafic and Mandy says, "The van performed brilliantly, allowing us down some very minor roads, where no others dared to tread. We used campsites every night, because we needed the heater on. We saw stunning scenery, day after day. We are very lucky to have all this a drive away, albeit a long one."

Manhattan owners Geoff and Jane went in the autumn, so they also wrapped up warmly and were glad of their campervan heater.

Shrimp their whippet loved chasing rabbits in the dunes at Dunnet Bay, and they saw dolphins from their camper at Chanonry Point, near Rosemarkle C&C Club Site.

At Applecross they were thrilled when stags joined them, laying down for the night between the camper and the shore.

While they were in Scotland the weather 'turned' and they battened down the hatches for a huge storm one night at Applecross. Fortunately it all blew over and they carried on with their campervan holiday in Scotland. Jane and Geoff recommend the NC500 route - but there were a few chilly days when Shrimp hid under the duvet, hoping nobody would see her.

EXPLORING
SCOTLAND'S
NC500

After staying local during lockdown, David and Karen made the bold decision to head from Dover to Scotland.

"We spent 17 days away and completed 2,367 miles, trouble-free. The campervan proved to be a comfortable abode and adequate in size for our needs. We did use an awning on occasions, for additional space, but this wasn't essential as we mainly experienced very pleasant weather for outdoor living."

"The highlights of our journey included magnificent scenery, wildlife sightings, pleasant walks, wild swimming and excellent Scottish hospitality. Now we are very much looking forward to further adventures."

Heading To Europe?

As well as taking advantage of the sights and activities in the UK, many campervan owners love touring campervan-friendly France, Portugal and Spain. Experienced travellers love to enjoy a more relaxed lifestyle, warmer climate and of course some of the regional culinary delights. There's a network of Aires de Services to try, as well as full-facility campsites in beautiful regions. If you have a good phone signal, Google will help you to find the nearest Aire.

Consider buying guide books to the Aires in the countries you will be visiting. For instance, you might choose All the Aires France North and South Together books or All the Aires Spain and Portugal, All the Aires Belgium, Luxembourg and the Netherlands, published by Vicarious Media.

The series is the original and best listing for these cheap and free camping spots for campervans throughout Europe.

Bobbie owns a VW Caledonia camper and she takes her dog Willow and cat Ebony with her when she escapes to warmer climates. She says, "I escape to the south of Spain during Britain's winter months, because, although there is some rain and it can be cold at night, most days are sunny and I can wear shorts all day, go to the beach, and sit outside to eat. The water is warm enough to swim in October and May but too cold for me from November to April. It doesn't stop my dog Willow from enjoying the sea most days. Food and drink is cheaper in Spain and I need less heating in my VW Caledonia than I would at home. Mostly I use Eurotunnel, and stay in the van with my dog and cat, but this year, I got the ferry from Portsmouth to Bilbao. A pet-friendly cabin meant my dog Willow and my cat Ebony were

EUROPE IN A SMALL CAMPER

In two years, Richard and his wife Hong explored 18 countries in their petrol-automatic campervan.

"On our first trip, we left Horsham in Sussex late in the afternoon and Rich drove all the way to Dover for three hours along the wiggly south coast roads. At the port they let us on the 11pm ferry to Calais. We even met another Sussex Campervan family waiting in the queue.

"We drove from Belgium on to Wertheim, Germany. German autobahns are scary as people go so fast. Even if you watch your rear view mirrors (which are very large and very good on the Nissan) cars come up behind you in a second! We arrived at a campsite by the River Tauber at Wertheim. After exploring, we got back to the camper at 9:30pm and quickly set it up for the night. We're finding this campervan so easy to convert from a car to a kitchen, to a dining room, to a bed!"

with me all the time."

In the first year of owning her Bamboo Green campervan, Sue and her husband Rick had already explored large parts of Europe. She says, "We picked the campervan up and went off for three weeks to France, Switzerland, Italy, Spain and back home through France. It was a very good trip and we stayed in an olive grove and visited a nice old hotel made from former stables at San Guiliano, near Pisa in Italy. After that we went to Spain to meet a friend who lives out there."

Suzi spent 2019 exploring Europe solo in her bespoke Sussex Campervan Lucy, a lovely purple Manhattan camper. She is now an expert in finding the best wild camping spots, and toured Scotland, England, France, Belgium, The Netherlands, Germany, Denmark, Norway, Sweden, Spain and Portugal in a campervan.

In June 2020, Suzi made a Covid 19 escape by ferry from Portsmouth to Santander and spent the first night in the misty mountains, at Torio. Her latest adventure had begun.

Then Suzi drove southwest, to the mountains of Northern Portugal, the Peneda-Geres, where the border was marked with a petrol station, a welcome sign, and the campervan clock whizzing back one hour.

Since then, Suzi has become a resident in Portugal and is planning to travel across the country. She documents her adventures on her YouTube channel, MindfulVanLife.

MINDFUL
VAN LIFE

EU Rules For Travelling By Campervan

The UK is no longer part of the EU. With that comes some changes to how we travel in and out of European countries.It is essential to know what the latest rules are and how they apply to you and your pets. A good place to start is www.gov.uk/foreign-travel-advice for current advice.

At the time of writing, these are the active EU rules for travelling by Campervan:

- Your Passport needs at least 6 months before expiry and be less than 10 years old (even if it has 6 months left) - this is also applicable to Switzerland, Lichtenstein, Norway and Iceland.
- You need to carry a valid driving licence and Green Card (proof of vehicle insurance available from your insurer).
- A GB sticker must be on display on the rear of your vehicle.
- It is worth having health insurance - your EHIC is valid until expiry and will then be replaced by Global Health Insurance Card GHIC.
- You can visit the EU for up to 90 days without a visa and spend no more than 90 out of 180 days there.
- Be careful what food and drink you take with you. Post-Brexit, you can no longer take any products that contain meat or milk into the EU and any of these items may be confiscated.

    Pet travel to Europe:

- You will need an Animal Health Certificate (AHC) from an official vet, which is valid for a single trip.
- All pets must be microchipped and vaccinated against rabies.

A Fine Day Out

Whatever the weather, campervans are perfect for days out and short breaks. Many owners say they use their campervan as a day van – or for short breaks - even more often than for longer holidays. Archaeologist Jenny uses her NV200 CamperCar as her only vehicle. She lives near beautiful Reigate Heath, in Surrey, and uses the camper to visit far-flung friends, or as a day van when she goes on archaeological digs. She says, "I went to Abinger in Surrey to see an archaeological site and cooked bacon sandwiches for all the people on the dig. They've come to expect it now. I've been out for plenty of picnics too.

Hobbies & Interests

Could you use your campervan to support your hobbies as well as for holidays?

Many people use campervans for festivals, rallies and events - but how many of us would actually set off in wild and wintry weather? Some of our friends use their vans all year round for a range of different activities, even finding that the colder parts of the year are their most active.

Stewart's first trip in his new Paradise Deluxe campervan was to the French Alps. "We stayed near La Clusaz in the Auvergne-Rhone-Alpes region of South-Eastern France. We went snow boarding and snow shoeing. I had no problems driving the campervan in ice and snow and the heater was very welcome."

Photo: Stewart

Stewart is also an instructor and assessor for the Duke of Edinburgh Awards and is a keen cyclist. Having a campervan has helped him to pursue his hobbies and explore further than he was able to before.

DAY TRIPS WITHOUT RESTRICTION

In 2020, during restrictions, Jeff and Mary used their camper as a day van for outings to Leonardslee Gardens, and going to their local Shoreham beach, with their grandchildren. "We parked by the fort on a glorious sunny day, went in the sea, ate in the van and it was brilliant. The toilet was very handy, too."

"We also like going to Seaford with our dog. She is a little Bichon Frise and has her own bed, seatbelt and a bowl hanging up in the campervan."

HEAD START ON ESCAPING LOCKDOWN

Families with campervans had a head start on escaping lockdown. They could travel safely between lockdowns, in their own little bubbles - allowing children to see their far-flung aunts, uncles, cousins and beloved grandparents outdoors, to create something near normal in this new topsy-turvey world.

For many, "getting back to normal" started with days out in the camper. In late spring Sussex Campervan owner Graham said, "I dropped the boys off at Thorpe Park for the day, then had a quick look at Windsor, before parking next to the Thames at Runnymede for a leisurely lunch and dog walk along the river bank. It felt like the first really hot day of summer, hopefully with many more to come. Our first proper use of the van this year, love it!"

By June, Graham and his family were off on a proper holiday to Sandford Holiday Park in Poole, Dorset, and the weather was glorious. It's a holiday park designed for families, with a swimming pool, pirate-themed crazy golf, sports dome and soccer school, plus a High Ropes Course for kids.

Illustrator Hugo and his wife Thea live in Brighton with their daughters Esther and Sylvia and dog Roller.

They collected their built-to-order Manhattan from Sussex Campervans last year and love it. They went to Devon's Croyde and Baggy Point this summer and Hugo says, "We go to Combas Farm campsite, Croyde. Thea used to go there as a little girl and we go every year. It's an amazing place with good facilities. It's a five-minute walk into Croyde, which has pubs and restaurants.

The main activity is surfing, from Croyde or Putsborough - a fabulous beach with a great cafe and views of Woolacombe. For us, rain or shine, it's the beach!"

SURF CAMPERS

Ian and Liz live in Cambridgeshire. Once they'd collected their campervan, they headed off to the beach for their first excursion.

"We cooked up a lovely breakfast overlooking the sea, just beautiful." said Ian. Later in the year they went to Tan Y Rhiw Caravan Park in Llanrwst, North Wales and explored the Cley nature reserve and beach on the North Norfolk Coast, before heading for the bright lights of Cromer.

BEACH LOVERS

HIDDEN TREASURES

Michael found a 1000-year-old Anglo-Saxon penny during one trip in his campervan.

"As a keen treasure hunter and landscape photographer, my campervan enables me to spend more time enjoying the hobbies I love. I'm out detecting every weekend and I often go away for rallies or trips with my local club. It's a fun hobby. In fact, I often say it's like Christmas, because you never know what you're going to turn up next. The oldest thing I've found dates from between 1500-2000 BC.

"I bought a campervan because it was the right choice for my hobbies and my lifestyle. My camper has made things so much easier. Now I can travel that bit further afield. Or if I'm out for the day, I have somewhere to relax with a hot cup of tea. It's great to be able to sit around a proper table and have a chat with friends."

FESTIVAL FEVER

Musician John and yoga teacher Julie love their red campervan.

John brought his guitar along when they collected their campervan and we realised that the interior needed somewhere safe for John to store his guitar to keep it safe on the road. He says, "The lovely people at Sussex Campervans fixed up a simple but effective little extra for me. I now have special straps attached inside and under the roof panel. Together they comfortably house my travel guitar. So when we stop for the evening, I'm generally entertaining the missus with a few songs, whilst she's usually knitting something for the many grandchildren now coming on the scene!

Steve's campervan helps him climb mountains.

"Spending a lot of money and ending up with the wrong van wasn't an option for us - so after much research, two visits to motorhome shows, poking around dozens of different vans and talking to many van people - we decided that a conversion based on the Nissan NV200 from Sussex Campervans was the one for us.

"We use our camper just about every weekend and holiday and it's my everyday vehicle too.

"It's a great vehicle to drive, both in town and at speed on the motorway. More importantly for me, it copes with the steep, narrow single track loads of the Welsh mountains and North-West Scotland, where it tucks very neatly into single passing places with ease. We spend a lot of time in these parts of the country. I've already climbed all the mountains over 3000ft in Scotland, England, Ireland and Wales, and everything over 2000ft in England and Wales. I've also run mountain marathons, and a van is great to use as a base camp for these kind of events."

As a wildlife photographer based in the UK, Mick regularly travels around the country photographing our Wildlife, giving talks to various societies and clubs and also running a series of photography workshops. However finding accommodation close to the venues could at times be a problem and costly, so in 2019 he decided to invest in a campervan.

WILDLIFE PHOTOGRAPHY

Whilst I use mostly commercial campsites, the campervan also gives me the flexibility to wild camp. It is ideal for this purpose, as very often I need to be in position and ready to start taking images well before dawn. Apart from using my van as a mobile "hide" I will also use my van on a daily basis to travel to my photography workshop venues. I take the van all over the UK, photographing various subjects from landscape to wildlife. I also travel to various clubs and societies, to deliver my series of photographic talks, using the van as my overnight accommodation.

Owning my Sussex Campervan has opened up new photographic avenues and has given me the freedom to explore the UK further afield, whilst keeping the associated costs to a minimum. It has also provided me with hours of fun and kept me occupied planning my trips, especially during the Lockdowns.

When Will You Take The Plunge?

Many people dream of owning a campervan for years and years before plucking up the courage to go and see campervans for sale.

Georgie and Nick live in Farnham and bought their campervan from Sussex Campervans three years ago, so I asked her if she had any advice for people thinking about campervan life:

Just do it!

It's the best investment we've made. We've had amazing holidays, and it doubles as our main vehicle for family outings."

Photo: Georgie

Photo: Tina

Photo: Heidi

Photo: John & Julie

Photo: Sandra

Photo: Rick & Sue